THE FREE CHURCH TODAY:
NEW LIFE FOR THE WHOLE CHURCH

The Free Church

Today: New Life for the Whole Church

BY ARTHUR A. ROUNER, JR.

WIPF & STOCK · Eugene, Oregon

Wipf and Stock Publishers
199 W 8th Ave, Suite 3
Eugene, OR 97401

The Free Church Today: New Life for the Whole Church
How a New Breed of Evangelical American Christians
can Electrify the Ecumenical Movement
By Rouner, Arthur A., Jr. and Kennedy, Gerald
Copyright©1968 by Rouner, Arthur A., Jr.
ISBN 13: 978-1-53264152-7
Publication date 9/27/2017
Previously published by Association Press, 1968

Introduction

There are times when great ideas and movements begin to run forward, and any criticism of them is regarded as either heresy or a spiritual hardening of the arteries. Sometimes later on we wish that we had listened to the criticisms. But at the time, the critics are shot down or are rolled over and crushed by the machine that favors the new. I have seen this happen in church conferences and I think it is now happening so far as what is vaguely called "the ecumenical movement" is concerned.

This great new fact of our time, as the late Archbishop of Canterbury, William Temple, put it, is certainly one of the most promising and exciting things in the Christian world. What has come out of the Second Vatican Council did not seem possible to me a few years ago. I never expected to see in my lifetime the Catholic-Protestant relationships which are becoming more commonplace every day. This whole new spirit of cooperation and appreciation is a miracle and the gift of God. What hath God and Pope John XXIII wrought?

Very few churchmen do not cheer this new ecumenical spirit. It is long overdue. All of us should understand that no single church has all the truth, that every communion has much to contribute to the whole, that denominational bitterness and competition are wrong, and that we must love each other and try to help each other in our common task of bringing the world to Christ.

Yet, when it comes to implementing these great hopes,

there is room for disagreement and there ought to be much discussion and criticism. Is one Protestant Church the will of God? Apparently Dr. Blake and Bishop Pike think so. Must that new church have bishops and be organized under episcopal authority? Arthur A. Rouner, Jr. has serious doubts about this one, and in this book he makes a very eloquent plea for the free church polity. This was very good for a fellow in the episcopal tradition to read and ponder. I have raised certain questions myself concerning the proposed merger of ten denominations. Arthur Rouner's voice should be heard and given honest consideration.

At the end of this book there is a rather simple plan suggested under the title "Proposal for Christian Unity." It is so simple that I believe it would receive approbation from the vast majority of Protestant Christians. It would be a definite step forward toward experiencing our unity and bearing witness to our essential oneness in Christ before the world. It would not water down our differences to some common denominator. It would not create a huge bureaucracy, which is nearly always the enemy of spiritual insight and experimentation. In short, it ought to be considered by all of us faithfully and honestly.

The trouble with a good deal of our discussion these days about ecumenicity is that it is in a vacuum or suspended in the air. It never gets down to the actual organization involved and what the cost will be in terms of church machinery. I belong to a communion that is very highly organized. Whenever I return from another high-powered church conference, I want to seek out the anti-institution brethren and volunteer to be their leader. I know, however, that churches must have machinery. I am not willing yet, however, to say that this can be increased a hundredfold and still provide the world with a great new Christian power. My guess is that Arthur Rouner has also had some of these misgivings.

At any rate, it seems clear to me that this ecumenical business needs great debate within an atmosphere where differences are welcomed. We ought not to say that a man is against the ecumenical movement because he does not get enthusiastic over some particular form of organizing it. Nor should we move forward without being aware of the great virtues of the past. The free church pluralism of America has provided us with the most relevant church life I know of anywhere. The good Lord knows it is bad in many ways and needs improvement, but not all of it is bad. Can we save the good and at the same time take another step toward the better? Before you make up your mind, it will be well to read and ponder the following pages.

BISHOP GERALD KENNEDY

Hollywood, California

Contents

Introduction by Bishop Gerald Kennedy • 5

Preface • 10

1. The Ecumenical Church and the Gathered Church • 19

    The gathered church . . . The gifts of the gathered church . . . The church behind the wall

2. The Gifts of the Gathered Church • 37

    The covenant idea . . . The pilgrim spirit . . . The church meeting . . . The free church . . . Of orders and the rest

3. The Faith of the Gathered Church • 47

    The theological dilemma . . . The theological situation . . . What the new ground of agreement cannot be . . . What the new ground of agreement must be . . . No creed, but a covenant . . . The essential faith

4. The Gathered Church and the Meaning of Ministry • 63

    The witness of one man's life . . . The gift of the Spirit: the key to the ministry . . . The ministry as a high and holy thing . . . The Holy Spirit and the apostolic ministry . . . The ministry of the people

Contents

5. The Gathered Church and God's People at
   Worship • 82

   The trouble with the church . . . The hunger for the Spirit . . .
   The gathered church and the power of the Spirit . . . The
   gathered church and its gift to great worship . . . Renewal and
   reform . . . Pioneers from the left

6. The Gathered Church and the Mission in the
   World • 100

   The contemporary debate . . . The fatal fallacy . . . The fallacy
   of the faith . . . The fallacy of the church . . . The gathered
   church as a vehicle for mission . . . The gathered church and
   the missionary concern

7. The Gathered Church and the Spirit's Power • 122

   The sense of the Spirit . . . The power of the Spirit . . . The
   gathered church as a vehicle of the Spirit . . . No gathered
   church, no unity

8. A Church for the World • 137

   The hope in the world . . . How can the walls come down? . . .
   What laymen are looking for . . . Some ways of organizing the
   great church coming . . . Removing the stumbling blocks . . .
   A new way for the church to try . . . The congregation as a key
   to the reunited church . . . The congregation as meeting ground
   and battle ground . . . A church for the world

Preface

One does not need to be a prophet or seer, I think, to read in the signs of the time that the days through which the church of Jesus Christ is living now are among its most exciting and significant. They are not its halcyon days; they are not its most glorious, as in the first century of its life; they are not its most dramatic, as in the sixteenth-century days of Reformation. But they are crucial days, days when every Christian counts, days that will tell the story of the future. They are great days to be alive in the life of the church.

They are great days because they are days of change—days of radical change, in form and structure, in theology and mission, and in the very stance and alignment of the church. Part of the excitement is that everything is changing. America is in the throes of a crisis in authority. In social life, in political and moral life, as well as in religious life the word of authority is less and less heard. Many have written about what seems to be happening to America's morality. It does not need to be documented here. Much too has been written about America's religion: about the exciting new "religionless Christianity" of Bonhoeffer, the "Honest to God" realism, and on to the "death of God" idea.

Some are excited because religion seems at last to have caught on, to have learned "the name of the game," to have caught up with the times. Many in the church hail the new thinking, and not a few clergy rise to meet what they think is the new tide.

Preface

I am one who thinks they misread the signs of the time, that they are missing what is most significant and what is going to make the most difference for the ages and ages hence. If the gospel of Jesus Christ is "the same yesterday, and today, and for ever"—and I believe it is—then the excitements of today will evaporate, and we will have spent our energies and thoughts on the things most ephemeral, and have missed the point of our period in history, unless we have eyes to see what is the real excitement of our time, and what is the most significant.

The real news today, I believe, is the life of the spirit. It is what the Holy Spirit is doing in the world in the most unexpected places.

One of those unexpected places is the Roman Catholic Church—everywhere. Many think Rome is getting the ecumenical spirit, preparing to organize with the Protestants into one big church again. I think what is happening to Rome is far more profound than that. I think the Roman Church is on its knees—in prayer, and before the open Bible. I think they are beginning to read the Bible as our evangelical friends long have read it, as the Word of God to sinful men. I think they are taking it seriously, and that the Bible, under the power of the Holy Spirit, is leading Rome on pilgrimage: on pilgrimage back to the days of the church's first century, back to the days before popes and politics, before church and state, and before cathedrals and colleges of cardinals.

What is curious and exciting to me and, I think, of vast significance to the future of the church, is that this pilgrimage through the pages of Scripture to the vitality and Spirit-dominated life of the church of the apostles is precisely the pilgrimage made in the late Reformation years by the first of the modern-day "free" churches, the "gathered" churches of the English Pilgrim or separatist movement of the late sixteenth and early seventeenth centuries. The Roman Catholic Church is discovering in our day what the Congregationalists and Baptists, forerunners of the Disciples, Covenant, Quaker, and Pentecostal traditions, discovered three hundred years ago.

I am convinced that many Catholics and many free church, theological conservatives, and evangelical Protestants do not realize it yet: we are moving into a day when these Christian groups, the very ones that have long thought of themselves as at opposite poles in theology and polity, are going to discover that in things of the heart and of deep belief they are the ones who have most in common. Dr. Billy Graham was mouthing no platitude when he admitted after his Boston visit with Richard Cardinal Cushing that he felt closer to some Catholics than he did to many of his Protestant friends. Well he might say so, for here in common is a sense of God's authority and man's sinfulness and need—and also, a growing awareness among Catholics of the centrality of the "Word" in worship, of the importance of the people, and of the freedom of the Spirit.

There is a new, common view of the nature of the church emerging, in which Catholics are sensing more and more that the church is, in the final analysis, the local congregation of the two or three gathered together by Christ, their absolute Lord, who governs by the power of his Holy Spirit.

Curious too, for the church scene today is that these two traditions—from the far right and the far left, in terms of church polity—are those least likely to be enamored of the very thing that many think to be the whole purpose of the ecumenical movement: the gathering of everybody, but everybody, into one vast organizational church. The free-church Protestants have too great a fear of what organization can do to the power of the Spirit, and the Catholics are realistic enough to know this would be too much to hope for from the free churchmen. In the meantime, their own pilgrimage is leading them to have some doubts about the infallibility of organization and centralization.

In the meantime, on the Protestant side, many conservative

Preface

and evangelical churchmen are themselves on something of a pilgrimage in their concern for social justice and Christian action. A new concern is rising, and men who long thought the two concerns were mutually exclusive are finding that a new conviction is emerging, the need for a new man, who is an utterly committed Christian in evangelical faith, but who at the same time—out of that faith—cares deeply about justice and love in the world Christ came to save.

These are movements of our time that excite me and tell me that God is doing something strange and wonderful among men in my time. Where they will end, I do not know. But that they have begun, I am utterly certain.

If this is true, I think we face a decade, and much longer, of great surprises. And if this is true, it also means that in a day when the Christian church, and indeed the Christian faith itself, seems to be fighting with its back to the wall against forces both from within and from without that appear bent on its destruction, there is hope of help from a new quarter, a new alliance—an alliance that could bring the answers from the Spirit of God which secretly this generation is seeking, and which could provide the key to the present-day ecumenical dilemma, in an emphasis on what the Holy Spirit can do, when organization fails, to bring men together in common work, at a common table, and under orders mutually accepted and recognized by all.

I pray God it is no arrogance that leads me to think this is an insight that has been given for sharing with all who might listen or read. It seems to me someone should say these things, even if only a few give heed. I am glad enough to be one of those to speak.

That is the reason for this book, and for the stolen hours and vacation days that have produced it. My hope is that some, at least, will find in it a truth, and that so it may give honor to the One whom all Christians know to be not only the Truth, but also the very Way and the Life for them.

Sometimes, in the midst of the pressures and demands of the modern ministry, the writing of a book would seem the last thing a busy pastor would want to undertake. Indeed, there are times when the agony of grinding out on paper one's deepest concerns in a form comprehensible to others seems, after all, to be hardly worth the effort. But somehow, like Francis Thompson's "Hound of Heaven," through all the labyrinthian ways of your own mind the idea pursues, and so you return to it—struggling to find the time, and striving to say what you feel so surely.

My concern is about what everyone knows today as the "ecumenical movement." It is about how that "great church" will ever come. It is about what it will be. And it is particularly about the contribution that the "free" churches in America will make to it.

There is no doubt about the fact that the ecumenical movement is here to stay. The word is known, if not understood, by Christians throughout the world. It comes from a Greek word meaning "whole," "universal," meaning the movement of all churches, and all denominations, and all Christians toward unity, toward standing together, and worshiping, and acting, and witnessing together as brothers in Christ. It means overcoming the differences that divide us.

That the ecumenical movement is valid and part of God's will for his church today is attested by the fact that suddenly, seemingly out of nowhere, the Roman Catholic Church has taken up the cry and the cause, and her heart is reaching across barriers the Protestant world had never dreamed to see bridged! There is no question but that Rome and her worldwide church has been deeply influenced by the thought and conviction of Protestant ecumenical theologians and statesmen.

But while Rome joins Geneva in the new cause of our time, my concern is for the large minority of American churches and churchmen who have remained almost untouched by the

Preface 15

new concern and the new hope. Not only have they not been caught up by it, they have sometimes been repelled by it. Skepticism and mistrust have led too often to misunderstanding. And this does not need to be.

Perhaps the people of these traditions do not realize that the so-called ecumenical movement is, or at least can be, part of that very mission and ministry of the Gospel in the world about which they are so sincerely concerned. But what is far more tragic is that they fail to see that they themselves, they personally, and their denominational traditions, have more to offer and are more vitally needed in the ecumenical movement than they had ever dreamed.

They have something, I am convinced, which the ecumenical movement needs desperately today if it is to live at all, if it is to avoid being swallowed up and consumed by mere ecclesiastical machination and machinery, and if it is ever to provide "a Way" for Christian brothers to walk together.

The churches I refer to, the people who concern me, are those of the "free" churches in America, those at the left end of the spectrum of American Protestantism. And by "free" I do not mean to make an odious comparison to some of the more traditional, liturgical, and more highly structured denominations. I mean simply those denominational traditions which have had either a freer and more flexible tradition of theology or a freer and more flexible tradition of polity. I mean the traditions not bound by creeds, or by specific theological formulations, or those not bound by liturgical or constitutional practice and law. I am thinking of the Friends, of the Baptists—Southern and Northern—of the Pentecostal groups, of the Disciples, and of the Congregationalists—my own tradition—both those who continue in the historic pattern and those who have gone on into the new tradition of the United Church of Christ. There are other groups who perhaps both should and would want to be included among these traditions—some of the Methodists, the Missionary Alliance churches, the Adventists, the Covenant churches, the Evangelical Free Church, and others.

These free churches, I am convinced, have far more in common with each other than they realize, and they also have far more in common with the ecumenical movement than they realize. While some of their denominational leaders have been immersed in the ecumenical movement as leaders, many of their own people have remained aloof and uncertain, and uncommitted.

My hope is that this book might help to show what tremendous gifts they have for "the coming great church" and why they are so needed; and also to challenge them to give those gifts, and to help the ecumenical church to accept them. I do this in awareness of my own failures here, but also with a sense of tremendous inner excitement at what the insights and understanding of the free church view of the church has to offer to the church ecumenical.

I am not beyond believing that the free churches may hold the key to the future of the coming great church, that they may have within their own life and practice the basis of new forms which can be the answer to some of the deepest differences separating Christians from each other today. I think they may be able to offer the freedom the ecumenical church needs, but also the basic commitment to Christ as a person that it needs. I think they may be able to offer the form and framework in which churches of vastly different tradition and background can work and serve together. And I think they may possibly offer an understanding of the church free from entangling ecclesiasticisms in the relation between churches, for which our world and its modern men are "hungering and thirsting."

Perhaps this will seem like news to nobody but me. Perhaps some will say the ecumenical movement has long since passed the point at which ideas such as these would be either useful or welcome. But they are burning inside me to be said, and

Preface

my secret prayer as I send out this book is that some will read and welcome its message, and perhaps even pass it on, and that it may serve, in some way, to bring into the ecumenical discussions and plans of our generation, or even of some future generation, a new force with a new insight and a new power that will make more profound and real the impact of Christ's whole church upon the world.

Without my wife's persistent criticism and encouragement, and her insistence that such a book was needed and must be written by me, these pages would never have been attempted or completed. And only with the loyal and dedicated labor of my secretary, Mrs. Lois Collings, in typing the manuscript more than once, would they ever have seen the light of day. I have also to thank Mrs. Muriel Buell, whose keen editorial eye could see and sure grip of the faith could reveal where the message was not getting through and who did what few can do, make the work of her friend make sense.

Others too numerous to name have influenced and inspired me along the way, through a word spoken here, a pamphlet written there, or a helpful insight picked up somewhere else. Particularly should I acknowledge the influence, through long conversations, of my Episcopalian sister, Elizabeth Stephens Rouner, Head of History at the Spence School in New York, and of the very diverse influence of those most precious men in my life, my father and my brother, who, for very different reasons, may be surprised at what is written here. Though we frequently have not agreed and though our concerns have at many points been very different, these two, my kinsmen, both ministers—my father, the Rev. Dr. Arthur A. Rouner, recently retired, of Cadman Church, Brooklyn, and my brother, the Rev. Dr. Leroy S. Rouner, Lecturer in United Theological College, Bangalore, South India—have been my tutors and my antagonists in things ecumenical. Finally, I should be unfair if I did not mention gratefully the people of the Colonial Church of Edina, in Minneapolis, who graciously have given me that extra month each summer not only to rest but to write, by the shores of Lake Ossipee among the hills of New Hampshire which I call home. It was in those months and by that lake that this book was written.

These all have done their best. If the book does not come off, the fault will not be theirs, but that of the one who said, only inadequately, what was so deeply in his heart to say.

Arthur A. Rouner, Jr.

Tamarack Lodge, Center Ossipee, New Hampshire

1

The Ecumenical Church and the Gathered Church

For years the ecumenical movement has given the local church a hard time. In seminary classroom, in denominational offices, at the world meetings, in the religious press, and on many a church bookstore shelf the local church has been "taking it" for a decade. All the sin of the church was centered here, all its failures to be "relevant" were exposed here, all the cynical hypocrisy, all the bourgeois self-satisfaction, all the failure to "be the church" in the world, was laid at the local church's door.

For a young pastor, just a few years out of seminary himself, to return to his alma mater to expound to a new crop of seminarians the wonders and joys of life in the parish, to tell them that the people of God really *do* come hungry to the church on Sabbath day, asking of their preacher "Is there any Word from the Lord?," that God's little ones *do* hunger and thirst after righteousness, that they want to serve their Lord in the world, and that their demand was constantly, "Sir, we would see Jesus"—why, this was unheard of! Could it *really* be like that? You mean, the people of the local church are not really theological nincompoops, mere nominal Christians with no real understanding of what the church and the faith were all about? The theological students could hardly believe their ears—and particularly from one of their own, because this is not what they had been taught. This was not the message that was getting through from their courses in theology and ethics and New Testament.

In the decade of the '50's, the local church had been considered by all hands to be the weakest link in the Christian church's chain of command. Live and function at the executive level, the cry was heard, and you can really *do* something: society can be influenced, public statements can be issued, "relevant" decisions can be made. But try it at the local level and you're lost! Indeed, the whole Protestant ecumenical movement, by the admission of its leaders themselves, has lived and moved and had its being almost entirely on the higher levels. Denominational leaders have felt that nothing gets done at the local level, and at least one prominent seminary professor has said that "the local church is incapable of making ethical decisions." The local church, obviously, has not been the "in" place to be.

And certainly the local church has not been considered to have anything of great significance to offer to the movement toward Christian unity. It has been consigned more than once, by the bright up-and-coming young theologians and socio-theological commentators, to the fate worse than death, called "irrelevance." And yet, with the birth of the 1960's the pendulum has begun to swing again. The local church is just beginning to get a hearing. Langdon Gilkey finds it no longer irrelevant to write a book on mission from the local church's viewpoint, called *How the Church Can Minister in the World Without Losing Itself*. George W. Webber, of the East Harlem Protestant Parish, does much the same in his *The Congregation in Mission*. And even Browne Barr can get away with a book called *Parish Backtalk*. The local church appears headed for a new day, but as yet few have sensed its significance for the ecumenical movement, that the church in its truest and most common form is the people of God gathered around Christ, not so much by their own will but by the drawing power of the Holy Spirit.

The Gathered Church

It is this idea of the church, this understanding of what the church of Christ most essentially is, that has been known among Christians as the gathered church. It is a New Testament idea. For if we turn to the Book of Acts or to the letters of Paul, we discover a kind of church life primarily *local* in its nature. No such thing as denominations existed then. A "church" was not an organization made up of local congregations. The "church" was either the whole church, the church universal, in all times and places, known and unknown, and made up of all those who belonged to Christ, living or dead—or it was a particular church, existing in a particular community, living and walking and having its mission and worshiping in a particular place: an identifiable company of very particular individuals bound together by specific commitment to Christ and to each other. The "church," in Paul's letters, was the church in Rome, or the church at Philippi, or the church in Corinth. Frequently it was even more closely defined as the church in so-and-so's house. Such it is in Colossians 4:15: "Salute the brethren which are in Laodicea, and Nymphas, and the church which is in in his house." Or in Romans 16:3-5: "Greet Priscilla and Aquila . . . likewise greet the church that is in their house."

Jesus had said, "where two or three are gathered together in my name, there am I in the midst of them." It was this emphasis upon the gathering power of the Lord Christ, working his works of love in the hearts of men, and drawing them to him, that was apparently the ruling principle of the form and growth of the church's life in first-century Christianity. The church was not all those nominally Christian people who happened to live in a particular geographic district. That is the parish-church idea that is followed today by the Catholic Church, the Anglican Church, the Presbyterian Church of Scotland, and presumably by all state churches.

The church was rather those whose hearts had been touched by Christ, sincere and committed believers, who had been led by his Spirit to become part of a particular congregation of believers by their own choice. They might live halfway across town. They might dwell in some other parish district. But they came to that church, they were part of that company of Christ's people because Christ, in his Spirit, had called them. He had "gathered" them.

Furthermore, as far as we can tell, there was no legal jurisdiction over them by any other person or by any other church or churches. They loved their fellow Christians of other churches in other towns, and they welcomed them eagerly into their fellowship when they were traveling through, but their life as a church was largely independent of other churches. Decisions were made by the whole church meeting together. Worship was led and guidance was given by their own leaders —a layman set aside, or a faithful pastor and preacher such as young Timothy.

The power and the authority which made those independent churches—the church in Rome or the church in Ephesus —to be true churches was the presence of Jesus Christ "in the midst of them." Jesus had promised that if they met faithfully in his Name he would be there with them, and it was the apparent conviction of the first-century church that the presence of Christ was sufficient authority to constitute a true church.

This historically has been the principle of the gathered church. It came into being again, after the long centuries of

The Gathered Church

medieval church life, in the late Reformation, in the Separatist churches of England, later known in England and America as the "Congregational" churches: "Congregational" because the life of the church centered on the *congregation*. Not, be it noted, individual independency, but mutual discipline, and love, and concern *in a congregation!* Here again, the belief that Christ was present with them in his Spirit was taken by these separatist churches of late sixteenth-century and early seventeenth-century England as sufficient warrant and authority to call themselves "churches."

It is this *gathered* idea that has been the fundamental principle of church authority that has characterized the life of the free churches in America. It is this kind of church, centering its life and mission in the local church, that will be meant henceforth in this book when we speak of the gathered church.

The Gifts of the Gathered Church

Is the local gathered church really passé? Is its day done and its usefulness outlived? Very few pastors of local churches would want to contend that there are no weaknesses there, no blind spots, no points at which the horizon narrows and the church's mission becomes fuzzy and indistinct. There *are* weaknesses, and they should be honestly admitted. And there are times when the intriguing idea of a church sociologist such as Gibson Winter, with his sector plans and institutional ministries, looks rather inviting as a substitute for the local church.

But what would there be—really—with*out* local churches? Would the group of Christians at a man's job really take their place? Would institutional chaplaincies, and executive offices, and theological seminaries, and quarterly meetings really take their place? Where would the healing of the fellowship take place? Where would men learn to live together in love?

Where, indeed, would the gospel be preached, and the church's mission be carried out?

Far from being an outworn and no longer necessary appendage of the Christian church in a new day, it is the local church which is the heart and life and nerve center of the whole church's ministry and mission in the complex and changing world of this exciting and significant century. It is the local church that lives at the grass roots of life. It is the local church that knows what is going on in local life. It is the local church that still has access to the husbands and wives, the children and parents of the fast-moving and fast-deteriorating American family. The local church is there: the local church is on the scene; the local church can, and is meant to be, the front line of the church's fight to win the world.

Surely it needs to be reformed and to be renewed. And yet, at the same time, it holds within its life the means and the power for the reformation and renewal of the whole church. A new day is coming for the local church: a day when its voice will be heard, and its word will speak true.

And should it not be that the local churches of every tradition should lead the way in making their gifts known to the whole church?

The spirit of the proposal this book would make is not to say that this is the only way, nor is it to say that all other ways are inadequate. It is rather to say that *this* way of the gathered church—by its very openness, and freedom, and yet its faithfulness and vitality—offers a form and a life in which all Christians, of EVERY tradition, could bear this witness with their own identity and their own uniqueness. The gathered churches offer a way not only toward unity, but also toward that reform and renewal that Christ's whole church seeks today.

And yet, as the mainstream of ecumenism has swept on, it would almost seem that in a few eddies and pools it has left its greatest gifts and its unique insights behind. I believe that this has happened: that men have gone ahead to meet the chal-

The Gathered Church

lenge of the ecumenical church, leaving behind, in some cases, their most powerful weapons, their most effective instruments for ecumenical encounter. And they have left them in the hands of those whose spirit has appeared to be, at the least, most *un*-ecumenical, most *un*-concerned about fellow-Christians, most content to carry on as things have always been done.

These persons left behind are those most full of fear about the ecumenical movement, most aware of its dangers, most frightened at its possibilities of power, most skeptical of its theology and purpose, and therefore most unlikely *ever* to venture forth bearing the good gifts left behind to offer to the brethren of the larger church.

"A place for me in the great church of the future?" they have protested. "Not on your life! I want no part of it." They have not dreamed that they have been left with a heritage that ought to be shared—that they are keepers of a kingdom that countless other Christians are seeking, that they have something powerful and unique and good that the whole church needs—that far from being the last hangers-on to a tradition that is dead, that has outworn its usefulness, that has no future, they are part of a glorious heritage that has the most real and relevant and needed message of all to speak not only to the ecumenical church but also to the world. The free churches stand dangerously near to denying their heritage and missing one of their greatest opportunities to serve in the world.

The Church Behind the Wall

Because, at least in relation to the movement for Christian unity, they have been a "fortress" church, a defensive church, a church behind battlements, a church protecting what it had, without daring to venture out into the unknown, taking what they had as a kind of "cause" to those with whom they disagreed.

Maybe they *knew* they had something of value. Maybe they felt nobody *wanted* what they had. But, in any case, they have hugged it to their bosom and hoarded it as a tiny light for their own edification but not as a flame held aloft as a beacon for the rest of the church.

They may say that the others have all departed the true faith, that they have forsaken the Gospel or forsaken the way of free faith—that all these others are not "true believers," or "truly Spirit-filled"—but underneath or along with this is the fear that should they participate in ecumenical discussions, should they get involved, and begin to know these people, and to work with them where they could, they would somehow lose their own purity, they would somehow compromise their own integrity, they would somehow become corrupted.

There has been no sense of *mission* in this area of their life, no deep concern for the ecumenical movement, no feeling that they, the free churches, had something great and wonderful and good that all these Presbyterians, and Episcopalians, and Lutherans, and Orthodox needed to hear about. In some sense they have not been sure enough about themselves, about who they were and what they stood for, and what they had to give in order to leave their battlements and go on the offensive and even mount a crusade to tell what they knew, and share what they had, and persuade their brethren to see and accept.

And to a larger degree this has come from the failure of the free churches to recognize that the need of our time constitutes a demand for the unique insights of the free churches. The very things the world is seeking for most desperately in the church today, those things the free churches have: at least by tradition, and heritage, and by original ideal and goal. I do not want to suggest that they have somehow captured the Kingdom of God while all the rest of Christendom has missed the boat; nor do I want to suggest that they are without sin or that they are even living up to their own ideals as they should. What I do mean to suggest is that in their heritage, in their

The Gathered Church

way, in the peculiar qualities of life which their forefathers sought to recover from the life of the New Testament Church, the free churches of today have inherited an insight, a way of looking at the world and of seeking God, a way of living together, a kind of concern that, at its best, comes very close to being the very insights, and concerns, and way of life that a whole generation of modern men are looking for in the church of today.

Do modern men want terribly to be recognized, to *be* somebody, to *count* in the world, to have a place, to escape the awful anonymity of a mass society in an urban culture, and be known by others and be *part* of a people? This is not easily given in the highly liturgical churches of our land, in the Catholic Church at the extreme where the concentration of the entire service is on the mass and its inner meanings, which depend so utterly upon what the individual brings to that service and on the hidden meanings he finds in it, and upon the special benefits that his own private soul may secure. This is why Catholic worship in America has tended to be *cathedral* worship with the value in the service itself and not particularly with the people's participation in it together. One lonely individual would be enough. Indeed, the service would go on even if *no* individual were there! The benefits of this kind of worship and atmosphere are *interior*. One goes largely to get something private for oneself. And the Latin which was long traditional enhanced that purely private nature; to a lesser degree other highly liturgical traditions—even where the service is "said" in English—tend to serve the same private sort of purpose. Very *little* sense is there here of the *corporate* quality of worship and of life. Very little concern is there here to be part of a whole people *together*.

In the free churches it tends to be the fellowship that counts; it is your place before God, not just individually but as part of a family, as part of a people. You belong to this company; the worship depends upon the whole company being there. You sing together, you pray together, you hear a sermon together—you are one people, and your "togetherness," your oneness of mind and spirit is absolutely crucial for the success and power of your worship. That experience touches lives because of "the brethren," because of the surrounding prayers and love of the whole company and not just because the service or mass is properly "said" by the priest or minister.

This means that the lonely modern man standing among that company counts for something. That is why he is often welcomed with a little extra warmth among the free churches; that is why the people there seem often to sense his presence just a little more than they sometimes do in the highly liturgical services. A man, hopefully, has a place among the people in free church life.

And the "free" churches frequently are concerned not nearly so much with statements of belief, but instead with the relationship of Christians with each other and with Christ. They commit men to a covenant, to an agreement to "walk in the way"—together, and with Christ.

And the free churches are committed to looking beneath the surface, to seeing the heart, and testing the Spirit. That is what the gathered churches are all about! About being open to the Spirit, about being ready at all times to be led by God.

Many are the unique insights of the free churches, the unspoken assumptions that have something to say to the whole church now at this very juncture in the ecumenical progress. There is their whole Pilgrim spirit, their view of the church as "gathered" around Christ, their sense of "covenant"—relation, the openness to the free movement of the Spirit among Christ's people—allowing for all the fullness of Christian experience in free prayer, in intercession. Their freedom is seen in their traditions of the free table and the free pulpit, of baptism as the concern of the whole people and not just the private few, of ordination as a thing of the Spirit and not of mechanics or pure rational choice, and of the place of every man as of supreme importance among the brethren without being just a name, or a "communicant."

The challenge that faces the Christian church today is profoundly and pointedly a quest for reality. Men and women are looking today for something that is "real"—something which rings true, which can be trusted, and depended upon. The young people say it with their question "Is it for real?"

And they want it in religion. They are hungering to find some church whose life and message and mission will speak to them about the real world as they know it, and about the real God who can save it. They are on the watch for sham and hypocrisy in the church, and when it's there they spot it every time!

But they are *there*—looking, and longing. And countless other people in our society who are not there are nevertheless watchful and waiting—watching and waiting for the church of Christ to do something or say something that will show that it cares about the real world and is really interested in the life and needs of that world.

But this is too often what men today are not finding in the organized church. They are finding the worst kind of superficiality and hypocrisy and sham. They want something of the heart, something from out of the depths of the Spirit. And yet they are given organization and more organization. They hear: "If we'll all just organize, get together into one great big thing, then we'll have something, then we'll win the world to Christ's standard!"

And yet it is precisely the organizational aspects of the church that most offend the world. It is the pompous parading, the symbols and ceremony, the precedents and prerogatives, the little rules and regulations—all the mumbo jumbo of ecclesiastical jargon and protocol that have turned the world away!

That is why the world—at least of young people—is listening to the folk singers first.

With a group of church young people once I sat at the feet of a folk song trio. They sang for nearly an hour, and we listened with a kind of awe. For, although they were only three young boys, they sang as if they had "been around," as if they knew the world they lived in, as if they had seen its sorrows, and knew its hurts, and shared its hopes. They sang with the poignancy and the sadness that have come to mark some of the greatest folk singing of our day.

Their songs asked questions that one cannot forget: How long will it be before a man will be recognized as a man? How long will it be until we see that battle is brutal and fighting is futile? How long must people live before they can be free? And how long will it take the rest of us to turn and see our responsibility? And with a kind of knowing wisdom of a secret knowledge beyond their elders' sight, they whispered that the answer is already "Blowin' in the Wind."

The songs were of the spirit, songs from the deepest soul of modern man. Yet they were songs you wouldn't likely hear in church. With a question that would be too embarrassing for many in the church. And they were being sung by three boys with no apparent connection with the church.

The folk song today is speaking to the people of our land. And it is speaking to them not because of catchy tunes, but because of what it is saying. It is reaching the heart of America in our time because it is singing the great truths and the great concerns of America in our time. It is speaking of the life and death, and the fears and hopes, and the defeats and dreams of American people. It is reaching America because it is real—because it speaks to people of life the way it is. It sings of that which is true, and they listen because they know it *is* true.

Reality. That is the song the people sing. That is the song they hunger to hear. And this is the problem of the church

The Gathered Church

today. The problem of reality. That note of authenticity, that note of the folk song they do not hear in the Christian church today. The reality they feel in the folk song is something they seem to miss when the church speaks. And they ask as T. S. Eliot asked:

> Where is the life we have lost in living?
> Where is the wisdom we have lost in knowledge?
> Where is the knowledge we have lost in information?
> The cycles of heaven in twenty centuries
> Bring us farther from God and nearer to the Dust.[1]

The world is asking if there is not something missing from the church today that should be part of its life, and should be heard in its voice. The charge against the church, again and again, is irrelevance. "You say good things," they say, "all nice—all true—but not really relevant. Not really words that make a difference. Not really words that change anything.— Not a word like the newspapers say, or like a university speaks, or like the law hands down. You are not in touch with the world," they say. "You do not speak about things as they are. We are a nation in ferment, and you have nothing to say, no action to offer."

And even for hundreds of people within a church it is doubtful whether the church is alive and vital and relevant for them. Many church families find that their church relationship is one they can take or leave. Their Bible is a closed book to them. Prayer is a lost art for them—even at the family dinner table. The church does not challenge them. It does not reach their heart. It is not really alive for them.

Organization, mechanics, legalisms never won a man's heart! They have their place but they have never been what made a man Christian. And in the highest level of ecumenical

---

[1] T. S. Eliot, "Choruses from 'The Rock'," p. 157 in *Collected Poems, 1909-35*.

church life today these things are not breaking down the middle wall of partition that separates Christians—not even the Christians who are most involved in the ecumenical movement, who go to all the World Council meetings, who most talk about it locally, but who are most demanding in the end that their pattern must be practiced, their form must be used.

Because not all the tinkering nor all the talk has yet touched some of the deepest gulfs that divide Christians from each other. Not all the new united churches, or Blake-Pike proposals, or multitudinous "conversations" have yet struck down the real barriers—the barriers raised by those denominations and Christians who believe that their "orders," their ordination for their ministers, are more valid than those of other Christians, that their communion is the only valid communion, and so do not welcome other Christians at "their" table.

The impatience with the church is real among many, and making the church more "churchy" by building up organizations of twenty million members replete with hierarchy and protocol—even in the name of Christian unity—will be dubious help. Another way is wanted: an open way, a free way, a way in which God's Spirit can move where it will without the petty limitations of man's pride, and pretense, and narrowness, and smallness of soul.

The "way" of the New Testament Church was uniquely the "Spirit" way. Those churches to which Paul wrote were not ruled by any ecclesiastical ordering from him or from anyone else. They looked literally to the Holy Spirit to lead them. By "Spirit" they meant the third Person of the Trinity—God the Holy Spirit, who was in fact the God whom they had come to know in Jesus Christ, alive and at work in their world. The Holy Spirit was the living God himself: unseen, untouched, but as real as anything they knew in life! The means of his power was his strange working in the hearts of men, moving them, persuading them, changing their minds, speaking to their inner conscience in such a way that they were led together into a oneness of purpose, a unity of action, and a curious new power that made all things possible to them. They were literally "Spirit" churches: churches invaded, infused, and overwhelmed by the intangible and yet real and recognized personal power of God.

Maybe the Bible has something when it says, "Not by might, nor by power, but by my spirit, saith the Lord!" Couldn't that be the answer? Is it not possible that the one thing missing in the church and in its movement toward unity is the Spirit?

The Church had it once. It had a Spirit in its life that gave it the touch of reality. And that is what modern men are looking for in the church today: the Spirit that can touch the heart; the Spirit that can move the soul; the Spirit that can speak to them of life and truth.

After all, it is only through the Spirit that the church can ever be itself. It is only through the Spirit that it can ever achieve any significant and meaningful unity. Only the recovery of the Spirit, then, and the attitude of looking-for and waiting-for the Spirit can ever bring about the unity and renewal for which the whole church is struggling and seeking. Only the Holy Spirit of God can break through all the morass of mechanics and make the church of Christ of one body and one mind and one heart and hand across all the differences that divide us.

This is what men are looking for everywhere in life today: something vital, something real, something to touch their heart. They are hungry for the Spirit. But Christianity has been offering them only the church. Holy Spirit has been losing to Holy Church. And the world is fed up with the church! The world has had all the "church" it can stomach.

The world wants *Christ* to come through—not a whole bunch of rules and religion and meaningless piety. The world wants the Spirit, not the church. It wants that certain something that one heart can give another: that quality of spirit that can leap over barriers between people. It wants that which no amount of legal compromising can do. It is tired of the tinkering, mechanical "Churchianity" which it instinctively knows is a substitute for the real thing.

And yet the free churches, by the nature of their "way," have always been concerned with the Spirit. Their purpose from the beginning has been to fashion a way that would be genuinely open to the Spirit, and capable of being led by Him. Now, I do not pretend that only here among people of the left end of Protestantism can the Spirit be found. No one has captured and caged God's Spirit. Jesus said that the Spirit moves where it listeth, and no man knows whence it comes or whither it goes. It is wild, free, unpredictable. It meets with faithful men wherever they are gathered together.

But in some places it is easier for him to be, easier for him to move: and that is where men are open and expectant, where the church gathers looking for him, waiting for him, wanting to be ruled and led by him. And in some churches this is not very easy. Some churches put church above Spirit. They are not eager to have the free, fast-moving unpredictability of the Spirit in their midst. It is too dangerous, too uncontrolled. So they set up limitations. They enclose the church's life within canon law, and prayer books, and ancient creeds so that things can be done "decently and in order."

But there are other churches where this is not so: other churches where the doors are open and life is free, and where the people depend upon and look for God's Spirit. And these, by tradition, are the gathered churches, the free churches. This is a gift the gathered churches have been given. Not something to be arrogant or boastful about, but something to be grateful for, something to feel privileged to share. Something of the covenant way, the Pilgrim way, the way of the Holy Spirit which is part of the heritage of the whole church.

The whole church of Christ needs it. And it has fallen to

The Gathered Church

the free churches to have preserved it, in some measure, for the whole church in our day.

The failure of the free churches is that they have not tried; they have not moved out together into the ecumenical melee to make their witness. It is a failure with which the church and the world would charge them, and would challenge them to overcome and rectify for the good of the whole church and for the good of the world it would hope to serve.

The challenge is there. Where is there a way for every church to find the freedom to be led by the Spirit into such exciting new ventures? Where is the church to find a pattern that will make possible not only inner reform and renewal, but also the unity for which so many seek?

I do not think the world is looking for a patchwork of answers. I do not think it is wanting just one bright spot here or a glimmer of understanding there, but all the rest still a darkness. I think the world is looking to the church for some abiding principle, some principle both of unity and reform, that can meet the challenge it is flinging at the church today.

The quest for reality seeks not a new program or another organization but some sign, just some personal, simple sign that the church cares—that ritual and liturgy and hierarchy are unimportant beside something of the heart that can slash through all the rest and say "Look, here is the real church. Here is the church that cares about you, the church that is ready to take a chance, to lose her life in order to help you. Here is the church that says 'to blazes with all the pomp and circumstance if only the heart and simplicity of the Saviour can come through to you!' "

The free churches have something—not everything, but something of vital importance for the whole church today. Indeed, the world is looking for many of the things which most concern them, for the very kind of Spirit and reality that mean much to free churchmen. And yet the free churches have failed to sense that they have any obligation to the ecumenical church, that they have a great obligation to others. They have not sensed their mission here, they have not really understood themselves and what a great thing they have to offer, nor have they understood that in a real sense they have a story to tell to the nations.

2

The Gifts of the Gathered Church

Here is the heart of all church life: the "gathered" idea, the idea of a living Lord who actually chooses men to follow him: "Come, follow me, and I will make you fishers of men." The idea is of a real Spirit and power that actually draw men together and make them a company of friends in faith, a people loving each other and held together by unseen ties for the purpose not only of helping and healing each other, but also of helping and healing and caring for the world beyond their little company.

It is the idea that gives divine depths to the hackneyed word "togetherness." This is what Christ came for, to reconcile men to God and to each other: to bring men into living, loving relationship with himself and with each other.

And this is what the whole Christian Church is about—about men loving Christ, and by that love being drawn together to work for the kingdom of Christ. ("Beloved, if God so loved us, we ought also to love one another." I John 4:11) This is why that pattern of church life all around the world, whatever the denomination, is the congregational pattern—the pattern of Christian people gathered together in local churches. Christians of diverse traditions have many forms and practices, and indeed some beliefs, that divide them from each other. But one thing they all have in common, one way of living they have all found meaningful and good, is the way of living the Christian life in local churches. Not all carry on the tradition of bishops, not all live by the rules of canon law, or worship by order of the Book of Common Prayer, nor do all baptize the same way, or ordain the same way, or take the Lord's Supper the same way. And yet the most obvious thing of *all* we have in *common*—congregations: local groups of people working and worshiping together.

And the gathered churches hold this as the most vital relationship. They claim this most universal form of life to be the most significant, the most important for Christians. What they have to offer the whole church is a form of life already most common among all churches. The idea of the gathered church is a unifying idea, an ecumenical idea, embracing all Christians everywhere, across all lines of geography, race, class, or country, and with global, international, world-wide concerns.

That united church has, in a sense, already resulted from the concern of many thousands to be one in Christ. Perhaps it is a kind of universal fellowship of the concerned. Yet always there is that certain future quality in people's thinking about it; that sense that a new kind of church—or perhaps a very old kind—is being fashioned, a church in which all Christians will have a closer relation to each other. It is that spirit of universal oneness which the New Delhi World Council of Churches was perhaps expressing in its "all in each place one" doctrine.

The idea of a "whole" church does not, I think, connote one single church organization. It does not imply monolithic structure. It could as easily imply a church of one Spirit, a church of common oneness, a church recognizing its own essential unity, a covenanted church with no barriers between —even though many vastly different forms of worship and life and even of organization might be contained within it. The idea carries with it a sense of openness, a sense of a new form

Gifts of the Gathered Church

of the whole church's life, a new kind of unity which is yet to be and which is even now being fashioned as the people of Christendom grow together.

The "Covenant" Idea

Part and parcel of the gathered church idea is the idea of the "Covenant": that men and women, called together by Christ, enter into voluntary commitment to each other as well as to Christ.

A covenant is an agreement—and in this case, an agreement among Christians that they will walk together in a certain way, that they will sustain a certain relationship with each other. The famous old covenant of the church in Salem, Massachusetts, promises:

> We covenant with the Lord, and one with another, and do bind ourselves in the presence of God, to walk together in all His ways, according as He is pleased to reveal Himself unto us in His blessed Word of Truth.

Here, the significant fact is the walking together, the relationship, the commitment to Christ and to each other. It does not say that they agree to believe the Christian faith in exactly the same way, or that they agree to believe all the same things.

Significantly, in interdenominational relationships today the discovery being made is that Christians of different traditions can like each other, love each other, and even work together, even though they do not in all things believe alike. And it is precisely this ability of the Christian spirit to leap over the barriers of belief by a relationship of the heart on which the gathered churches capitalize.

Here is the fundamental error of the more authoritarian churches. Their emphasis in church membership is in requiring right belief rather than right relationship. If you believe the right things, if you accept the Apostle's Creed, or the

Westminster confession, or some other right formula of doctrine, you are acceptable.

But, of course, even Jesus did not ask this of his disciples, when he called them to be his followers. Living in a relationship of love with Christ and with each other is what the gathered church asks of its members. It offers to the whole church the very path, through all the theological differences and suspicions of our time, which Jesus seems to have chosen in his. Not, "Believe just as we do," but, "Love the Lord you already know and walk with us as you follow him!"

How very different and how very important, if a way is to be found for all Christians to be of one company, in our day.

The Pilgrim Spirit

The gathered church in our country holds the Pilgrim spirit very dear.

The Pilgrim spirit came to America with the Pilgrim Fathers when they landed at Plymouth Rock in 1620. And it was the very spirit of the Bible which they tried to follow. It was the spirit of the seeker, of the man like Abraham, going out to a new country which he had never seen, because God sent him. It was the spirit of all the saints whom the book of Hebrews records as being "strangers and pilgrims" who "seek a country."

There is a certain restlessness in the pilgrim spirit, a certain seekingness, a certain openness, a certain sense that things are not entirely settled, that one must still be looking, still be keeping an open heart, still be searching for answers, still be scanning the skies for a sign, still following, learning, growing.

Rather a different spirit from that of some Christians and some church traditions who think they have found all the answers, that they have learned all the truth. The truth is in Christ, and he bids a man be a follower, be open in his heart, be a seeker—a member of the company, a troubadour on the highway of the Lord.

This view has profound significance for the theological discussions and differences of our time, for the pilgrim spirit has about it a certain sense of humility, as well as openness, a certain sense of searching, as well as knowing the truth. The pilgrim does not really need a creed because his whole purpose is to follow the living Christ wherever he leads, and to learn of him.

Perhaps this spirit, and this openness, and this commitment to follow—together with others—is one of the gathered church's greatest gifts to the whole church.

The Church Meeting

But how do the gathered churches "follow"? What means do they have of learning what the Spirit would say to them, of hearing his Word for their lives, of really being a company of Christians under the discipline of the Spirit? For many of these traditions what that means is the "Church Meeting": the church, that is the gathered people, literally "meeting" together to pray for and expect the guidance of the Holy Spirit as they lay before the Lord and each other those concerns which demand of them decision.

This is not the way church government works in the other great traditions. There, one man or small groups of men make the basic decisions. Yet, among the gathered churches it is the whole people, meeting together in prayer and in open honest discussion, who make the decisions of the church. And this is not unlike the early church's pattern where the people had "all things in common," and made their decisions in common.

It is a slow way, of course. But it is always slow convincing every one of a group that a certain action is right. Government by small, select groups (at least in churches) is a way of circumventing the masses, the crowd, and doing things more quickly, but it is also a way of losing touch with the people. And it is precisely this that many church hierarchies have discovered about themselves—that they have lost touch with the people. The Church Meeting is a way of keeping touch with the people.

But perhaps even more important than simply being the means by which the Holy Spirit guides his church, or a means for keeping touch with the people, is the fact that the Church Meeting is a means of reconciliation. For here the majority deliberately limits itself until all can be of the same mind. The intention is to work for unanimity in decisions. In most American institutions (and very often in churches) someone always "goes away mad" because the decision did not go his way. But when in the Church Meeting the majority will not act until all are convinced of what is right, there is no one left to go away mad.

This theory of "the gathered church" actually exalts the individual, making each man present important, whether he be butcher, baker, or candlestick maker. He is important because he is a child of God, and because God, in his Spirit, may choose this man through whom to speak his Word to the whole company.

This is the place where anyone can speak. This is the place where the newest, or youngest, or most insignificant member has fully as much right to speak as does the prominent person of long standing. This is the church meeting, the whole church.

And the reason why each member is important, the reason why he is significant, and why his word counts, is not because the gathered church is democratic, or because the members are fair-minded, or because "everyone should have his say." It is because what the meeting is seeking is the mind of Christ. It has gathered for the express purpose of so listening that it will be able to hear Christ's word, of so humbling its own will that it may begin to sense Christ's will, of so laying aside its

Gifts of the Gathered Church

own heavy hand and preconceived ideas of "what ought to be done" that it is able to be led in Christ's way. And Christ's word is spoken through the people's word, Christ's will is made known through the people's will: when they have prayed, when they have humbly sought God's guidance, and when they have listened and begun to hear him speak.

In this world of anonymity and "impersonal-ness" in human relations, here is offered a profoundly daring way of conducting human affairs, which makes individual responsibility significant to the whole people of God.

One of the most effective means of giving the church to the people and of recognizing the people as the church is the tradition of the Church Meeting.

The Free Table

One of the deepest divisions of the church today is the division it suffers at the very point at which Christ intended it to be most united: at the table of the Lord's Supper. It is not necessary to rehearse the differences and the divisions; they are evident.

And they have come into the church's life out of a feeling that some men were more holy, more consecrated, more properly set aside to give the Lord's Supper than other men. That is, that the ministers or priests of one tradition were more "of the truth" than those of other traditions and that therefore the sacrament they offered to Christian people was more valid than that offered by priests and ministers of other traditions.

But the gathered church holds no such view. The Lord's Supper is a sacrament, they say, at which the Lord presides. And it is his privilege to call whom he will to sit down with him. The invitation is extended to all men who love the Lord Jesus to gather at the table. They offer a table with no barriers: a free table.

In the traditions of most of the free churches, which see the local gathered church as containing within itself the fullness of the church, the sacrament of communion is far more important than many more liturgical churchmen have realized.

It is that experience of common worship in which Christ promises peculiarly to come and be truly and actually present with those who meet in his name. Because of this deep conviction of the reality of his presence through the Holy Spirit they have not felt it was for them to protect the integrity of the Lord's Supper—as long as they met "in his name," faithfully. Because if he was present, he would call whom he would to share the bread and cup with him. He would touch the hearts of those who were ready. In this sense, free churchmen have understood the communion table to be a free table: a table free for all men to come who love the Lord Jesus.

Because Christ is the true host at this sacred meal they have not accepted that only certain persons—whether ordained by bishops in Anglo-Catholic tradition, or ordained by their own free fellowship—could administer the Lord's Supper. *Any* committed Christian man or woman who was in covenant relation with his fellow Christians could serve the bread and wine to his friends and consecrate the bread and cup to holy use. Many lay members of the Disciples of Christ churches have their own communion sets.

This is the sacrament that was meant to bind Christians together, not to drive them apart. The free table, then, is open to all who love Christ, in order to draw them close to each other and to their Lord without barrier or hindrance. It is a reconciling, reuniting, ecumenical principle.

And because the free churches welcome all men, they conceive the sacrament as a rite of all the people: a sacred supper served in their midst, and served by Christ as the host. Therefore the table stands in the open with the minister behind it, facing the people, and they themselves gathered around it, at least symbolically, as one family.

Gifts of the Gathered Church

Even the Church of Rome is moving back toward the "table" from their altar; toward a view of Christ in the midst of his people, with the priest therefore facing his people. For the sacrifice of Christ was made once and for all in his death on the cross. It is not made over and over again on an altar, by man. What Christ did with his disciples was to eat a supper. And if we do it in remembrance of him it is not a sacrifice we celebrate, but a supper. Who knows but what some day, with this growing understanding, our Catholic brethren may offer the sacrament to all Christians, and that the table shall become a point of unity and not of division?

The gathered church offers to the whole church the heritage of a free table and an open communion.

Of Orders and the Rest

And what shall we say in so brief compass of so much else? Liturgically the sacrament of baptism is coming to be recognized as a public profession to be made in the midst of the whole family of the church. And here again, the free churches have preserved the way to which some of the liturgical churches now are turning. For it is in the center of the church, in the midst of public worship, that the sacrament is observed and the church plays its part, sharing in the promises, making the responsibility for Christian growth its own.

Even free prayer is a heritage the whole church is beginning to appreciate. For as it follows more and more the leading of the Spirit, it finds that Spirit not bound to prayer book form, but ready to use the free ideas of a man's glowing heart. So, for the liturgical revival, the free churches have preserved a certain openness before God's Spirit, at the holy time of the people's prayer, which the whole church greatly needs.

But at the heart of it all is the question of the authority of the church, and who guards its traditions, and teaches its way. There's the rub! Can a bishop's hand make a man of God?

Not the bishop without the Spirit! And the free churches have had no bishops, no physical succession of the apostles. Yet succession there is: the succession of the Spirit—of the Spirit of Christ in all his servants—in the whole people of God. And it is upon this Spirit alone that the gathered church wants to bestow the "orders" of its ministers. A Spirit given not by hands, though the hands of all the brethren are laid on, but a Spirit given by God's love through the heart. It is the evidence of this for which the free churches look, the power of this in a man's life that make him a minister of the Word, and a pastor to the people.

As the whole church opens its heart to the power of the Spirit, in spite of his unpredictability and the inconvenience he causes man, perhaps it will see that the gathered church has a gift indeed for all ministers of the church: the reminder that our power is not in the form or the ritual, but in the heart and the spirit—a reminder and a way that could break through the highest ecumenical barrier of our day, to provide a new way for a new day.

This is the excitement, and the hope, and the dream of the gathered churches. It is an excitement and a hope and a dream born of the knowledge that they have a secret, a special, wonderful gift to give to their brother Christians across the whole wide range of the church's life.

3

The Faith of the Gathered Church

There is no gift of the gathered church more crucial to be given than the gift of faith.

A proud boast that must seem! "Faith!," I can hear the great ecumenical churches saying with dismay, "Tell us you bring anything to the ecumenical movement but that! An open polity, a democratic spirit, a strong place for the laymen, an honored place for the local church—all these you may have, but don't tell us you come offering 'faith'! How can you presume to say it—you, with no great confessions of faith, with no reputable or scholarly theologians, and with every local church fashioning its own faith? Talk to us of anything but of faith, and of theology!"

Ridiculous it must seem for church traditions embracing such diversity of thought to say they have a gift to give in the realm of faith! And yet any fair understanding of the tradition of these far-left churches of the American theological spectrum would demand a hearing for their peculiar contribution to theology—and most especially to the theology of such an obviously ecumenical day.

I do not mean for a moment it is offered in any arrogant or self-righteous way. Those of the free church tradition would be all too quick to recognize that their tradition has not generally been associated with theology and theologians. This concern has seemed much more the prerogative of the more authoritative churches of the liturgical traditions.

But for better or worse, every Christian is a theologian, and every church, of whatever background, engages in theology. It is the plea of this chapter that the great ecumenically minded churches look carefully to see if perhaps it is not from the unsuspected Nazareth of the gathered churches that a key comes to break open the theological dilemma of our ecumenical day.

The Theological Dilemma

That we are, indeed, faced with a theological dilemma in this day of greatest ecumenical ferment is, I think, without question. More than at any time in the last four hundred years of the church's life there is a longing to be one, a deep desire to show our common unity in spirit, our oneness in Christ. But it does not *seem* so because, paradoxically, at the time of greatest desire, we are faced with the deepest gulf of separation. And particularly is that gulf opened wide among those church traditions which, on the surface at least, are apparently most concerned about finding unity and seeking ecumenical rapprochement.

It would seem that their very theological sophistication has become their ecumenical barrier. They deeply sense the "sin" of division among the churches, and yet they, of all traditions, cling most tenaciously to ideas that divide them from other Christians. They want a common ministry but do not recognize the valid ministries of the Spirit in other traditions. They want a common access to the Lord's table for all Christians, and yet again their exclusive view of the ministry prevents many of them from acknowledging the truth and power of the administration of the Lord's Supper in the freer church tradi-

Faith of the Gathered Church

tions. Their faint suspicion of others not of the same faith and practice becomes the very barrier on which the ecumenical enterprise founders today.

The Theological Situation

Yet curiously this is a denominational problem. It is not the problem of the independent theologians on the independent faculties of modern seminaries. It is the problem of long-held positions of denominational church bodies, of organizations of churches that hold funds together, and carry on programs together, and support missions together, and pay executives together, and have held certain theological positions and theological beliefs over many years and for many generations together.

And though these denominations seem stronger than ever, though their official positions in favor of racial justice and social concern and mission to the secular city would seem to put them in the vanguard of the great movements of our time, there is noticeable already the beginning of impatience with the denominational stance, the heavy machinery of denominational apparatus, the slow-moving process of denominational decision, and even the bureaucratic mind-set of denominational executives. Men in the field, men out in the church where the fight is on daily to win the minds of modern men, are not likely to have patience long with the back-stage struggles and the open floor fights of the power struggles of denominations. Whether it be Peter Berger raising the cry in his *The Noise of Solemn Assemblies*, or Stephen Rose making pointed jibes in his *Who's Killing the Church?*, criticism of the tendency of large structures of the church's life to heavy-footedness is growing.

Instead a new kind of concern is coming from the younger thinkers: a concern not wedded either to the old structures or to the old ideas. It seemed to begin with the "Honest to God" debate and the disturbing thinking of the almost despairing Bishop of Woolwich, John Robinson, who found the old ideas and the old forms no longer communicating to his friends in England, and who demanded a new way of looking at God and his church, a new attempt for relevance to the mood of our time.

And others too have taken up the cry. A neo-liberalism grows in the church. New voices drown out the voices of the great who held the stage only a few years ago. Their word is "relevance." They want the church to speak in the parlance of the time. They want to see her "communicate." They want her to be open to what the artists are saying, and the playwrights are saying, and the novelists are saying, and the folk singers are saying. They want the church to speak to "the secular city" and to listen to what the secular city is saying. They want her to move out into new forms of ministry, new ways of reaching people. They want the church in the supermarkets and in the hospitals, in the night life and in the half-light, in the factories and the offices—in a million places where they feel the church has never been.

The question here is not whether they are right, but whether they have the ear of our time—and they do. They have lost patience with the old ways and the old structures, and even the old beliefs. They want a new spirit, a new openness, a new daring to try new things.

They are the new voice of "the church"—the new theologians. And almost to a man they speak from outside the denominational structures. They are George W. Webber and William Stringfellow speaking from East Harlem, they are Robert Spike, who spoke from the National Council of Churches, and Harvey Cox from Harvard Divinity School, they are Don Benedict from the Chicago City Missionary Society. They are the voice of all those who have lost patience with everything static about the Christian church. They are the ones who look for God through the eyes of a kind of process-theology, as a growing, changing God.

And yet the old barriers, the old walls of exclusion are still held fast—paradoxically often by those who cry loudest for ecumenical advance. And in the midst of this is the new stirring, the increasing impatience to break through, to "be the church," to minister where the world really is, and to proclaim a Gospel the world can really understand.

Who has a way through the dilemma? Who has a key to unlock all these concerns, and to pioneer the way in which all Christians can stand together in love and power?

Listen to what the free churches, the forgotten churches, the churches of the gathered tradition dare to offer to the fashioning of an ecumenical faith.

What the New Ground of Agreement Cannot Be

Let first this warning be sounded: Be it understood on all sides that no neat compromise will do. The mood among many is that too much of that has already been done. All kinds of tinkering can be tried with that which is purely ecclesiastical machinery. But the deep convictions of mind and heart about God and his nature cannot be trod upon and turned into an easy compromise.

Men may be willing to give up a long-held and precious tradition of polity or practice, but they cannot be asked to give up their God and their knowledge of him just to make an attractive merger with another denomination possible.

No man, or denomination, or group of church traditions can presume, I think, to step into the ecumenical situation of today and offer a new creed or a new confession and seriously imagine it will be accepted by all the major church groups.

For long years the emphasis on mergers of denominations has accentuated the call for what some Christians view as a compromise of faith. Surely, the Roman Catholic Church—for all its new spirit and exciting dialogue—is not interested in compromising with anyone. It is seeking to renew its life from what it can discover out of the vitality of the early church's experience. It wants something in keeping with its long tradition and yet new and vital and relevant to the day in which the church now finds itself.

Nor yet surely are we to find the theologically conservative churches of American Protestantism interested in any sort of statement binding them to an expression of the faith which settles for anything less than the great doctrines which they have fought for as the truth.

No such proposal as this can ever win. Nothing based on compromise can possibly be an instrument in unifying either in spirit or in body the great moving forces of the Christian church today.

What the New Ground of Agreement Must Be

But without compromise, what is left to offer the churches as a basis for unity? Is one tradition simply to overpower another? Shall one tradition be accepted as the best middle ground and all agree on that? Or are the conservative traditions to insist that theirs is the only view and that we must all see it their way if we are to find the truth? Clearly, the imposing of one theological conviction upon all the others is no answer either to the ecumenical need of today.

The new ground of agreement must be positive, and it must be powerful. It must have integrity, but it must allow for variety. Moreover, it must be basic to the tradition and belief of all the great Christian groups. It must capture the heart and center of the faith on which all traditions already agree. And it must grow out of a past which all share.

Inevitably, this turns us, in our search, toward the faith and life of the first-century church—the church whose faith and life we find recorded in our New Testament: the New Testament which, obviously, the whole church shares.

It is to the life of the New Testament church that every church tradition of the Protestant Reformation turned in search of a pattern for its unique witness. Curiously, it is to that same seedbed of the first-century church's life that the Roman Catholic Church, in its period of renewed life and thought today, is also turning. In liturgy and in its understanding of the church, the Church of Rome is making the same pilgrimage that the churches of Geneva, and Wittenburg, and Edinburgh, and Scrooby made three hundred years ago. Perhaps its pilgrimage can be the same in the quest of faith?

Some pattern of faith then, true to the New Testament and its first-century church, can produce the only possible ground of agreement for an ecumenical faith today. Such a faith, surely, will grow out of the experience of the apostles, and will be of all things an open, growing faith—a faith humble enough to admit there is more to learn and know, a faith willing to keep searching, keep seeking, and keep open.

Who has had experience of that kind of faith? Who has tried to formulate the faith in any way like this? Who has managed to keep from settling down comfortably into a creed, and yet tried, at the same time, to maintain the essence of the Biblical belief?

The free churches, the churches of the gathered tradition, would humbly submit that this has been their "way." Not a "way" always faithfully followed: indeed, a "way" too often forsaken and lost, and sometimes not even understood. But a "way" nevertheless cherished over three hundred years as an ideal to be striven for. Its faith was held always in freedom but its trust was to be true to the apostolic experience from whence it came. See then, if the gathered church does not have something good to give toward an ecumenical faith.

No Creed, But a Covenant

For the churches of the gathered tradition, when it comes to matters of faith, there is something even more important than "right belief" or "right doctrine." In many churches the whole basis for church membership depends upon your believing the right things. Chances are you must believe them according to the formulation of the particular creed or confession which that denomination accepts. You are asked to say: "I believe in God the Father Almighty, Maker of heaven and earth . . ." and so on.

But Jesus never asked anything like this when he called Peter and Andrew and James and John to be his disciples. His only word was: "Come, and follow me."

He was saying, in fact, "I don't ask your theology, the things you believe right now. I ask your life. I ask your willingness to follow me: to be led and guided, your willingness to be seekers after the truth. I ask you only to be followers, to be pilgrims, to be seekers—men who are committed to walking together along the road of faith which I shall show you."

He asked from them only an agreement to be true to him and true to each other, in seeking to follow the Christian way. This is what a covenant is—not a mere statement of a faith already held, but an agreement to be part of a fellowship of people who are seeking together to grow into a greater faith.

A covenant is an open, live, and growing thing. It comes out of the pilgrim idea—the idea of being strangers and sojourners seeking a country—a heavenly country. "Abraham set out for the land of Canaan not knowing whither he went." And, as William Bradford wrote of the Pilgrim Fathers at the time of their departing for America at Delftshaven in Holland:

> So they lefte that goodly and pleasant citie which had been their resting place near twelve years. But they knew they were pilgrimes, and looked not much on those things, but lifted up

Faith of the Gathered Church

their eyes to ye heavens, their dearest countrie, and quieted their spirits.[1]

They did not know where they were going, but those people knew that they were going in the company of Christian brothers, and that God would guide them.

The covenants of many of the gathered churches contain the same simple emphasis upon a relationship with God and with brother Christians.

This covenant is a commitment not only to follow the Lord, but to follow him in company with a very particular band of Christian brothers. Men agree to love God, but to love each other also—surely not always an easy task, even among Christians!

This means that a "covenant people" are something more than a group who agree to believe the same things. They are a people who have entered into relationship, who belong to each other, who are brothers.

The essence of such a relationship, of such a way of conceiving the Christian faith—as a commitment to accept Christ, to follow Him, and to walk with others who also follow Him—is an attempt to make room for and to exalt an essential element of the Christian experience: love.

Things can get so complicated in the Christian church, what with all the intricacies of theology and polity, that sometimes we forget that something as simple as love is still basic, still the basis of the whole Christian life. In fact, what Jesus on the last night of his life tried to say to those he loved the most was: "They won't even know you're a Christian, unless you love one another!"—"A new commandment I give unto you, that ye love one another; as I have loved you, that ye also love one another." Indeed, this more than anything else is what convinced the first-century world of the power of Christianity: "See how these Christians love one another!"

[1] *The Pilgrim Reader*, p. 76, George F. Williams.

The form in which that love is often expressed, the way in which it is exercised in discipline and in faith, is through this concept of the covenant. This is essential to the tradition of any growing, seeking, expanding faith—a tradition that cares a lot more about where you are going than about where you have been, a lot more about the spirit in your heart than about the law in your mind, a lot more about the love with which you live than about the "articles of faith" which you say that you believe.

Somehow, this emphasis on following Christ, on commiting yourself to him personally, and agreeing to go wherever he leads, no matter into what new truth or new relationship it may lead you, and then agreeing to accept as your brothers those who also love Christ because he has accepted them, strikes close both to the New Testament demand for faith and to the deep hunger to believe.

Men today are not interested in the theological squabbles of the seminaries or the denominations. They hunger for a relationship: a relationship with a living, loving Person who can save their lives. And if the New Testament record does not betray us, Christ himself was interested not so much in a man's theology as in his willingness to be a follower, to enter into relationship, to take the first step of spiritual pilgrimage, to seek and grow into new truth, as he would lead.

In a sense Jesus was saying, "Leave your theology to me. I will lead you into all truth. Be patient. Be willing to follow, to grow, to develop. I do not want you to think you have the whole truth. Be humble. Be prepared to wait and grow. If you will live and learn with me you will have a complete theology all right, and it will be your own. Your own experience, your own knowledge—of me. Just be a disciple now, a follower, and take me as your Lord!"

Perhaps this is why the only creed of the New Testament church was the great affirmation: "Jesus is Lord!" Just that. Just that one simple testimony. Jesus as Lord of your life in almost any way you understand Lordship. Lord of all you are. The one you obey, the one you follow, the one you love.

It is by emphasizing the personal relationship, the quality of growing and becoming, the pilgrim quality of movement together along the road of faith, that so much of the theological subtlety and nuance implied in a creed, with all its temptation to division, is done away. And yet individuality and difference are not done away. Integrity and power as well as variety and individuality are maintained.

The covenant idea offers a basis for unity in theology for Christians all across the theological spectrum. The diverse traditions of Christendom have much on which they differ. And yet, all along the line they have deep truths which they share, and deep affections for each other as persons which now are possible as they once were not. The essential thing is to know Christ, and to follow him if they can, together. This the covenant-relation makes possible. The gathered church offers the whole church this gift toward the fashioning of a united faith.

The Essential Faith

But what sort of faith does such freedom fashion? Is it a faith that can be trusted? Does it foster heresy or can it foster truth?

This could be a real question both for biblical conservative and for orthodox Catholic. It is a question that should be answered if any claim is to be made for an ecumenical faith.

Does the covenant idea lead to a faith that could win the approval of the great denominations of today? The free churches would answer with a hopeful "Yes!"

The great temptation of denominations is to believe there can be no variety and still have truth; no variety and still have love; no variety and still be united.

The essential witness, perhaps, of the free churches is to show the theological world that there can be unity in spite of diversity, that there can be love even with individuality. The heart of the matter is to agree on what is essential, what is basic, what is the core, and not to worry about variety in the rest.

Of course, that has been the stumbling block for Christians of differing traditions: to agree on what *is* essential in "the faith." And yet, it is remarkable how few of the great claims of the great denominations have to do with this essential belief about the God they have all come to know in Christ. Whether it be the congregational autonomy of the free churches, the authority of presbytery among Presbyterians, the office of bishops in episcopacy, or the form of baptism among the Baptists, none of these are essentially of the faith. They really are matters of polity, of ways of structuring your life after you are a Christian. The essential of the Christian faith is Jesus Christ, risen from the dead. What he called men into was a personal relationship with him, a following and walking with him *together*—that is, with those others whom he also calls. It is to this, and to this alone, that the covenant relationship calls men.

The way of the gathered church has been (many would say from the New Testament day itself) the way of free men under Christ. It has been their conviction that what Christ demanded of one man in his way of worship, in his acts of service, and in his testimony to the faith was not necessarily what Christ asked of another man. We are one body, yet many members, as Paul said, one people, but with differing gifts. "Now there are diversities of gifts," he said to the Corinthians, "but the same Spirit."

But by no means has this meant a matter of every man for himself in the things of faith! The faith of free churchmen has not been a flaccid, facile thing. We may have lived through changing times, and through many shifts of the theological winds. But never have these churches quite lost touch with the heart of the faith. They have never forgotten

Faith of the Gathered Church

the Gospel. They may say it in new ways. They may sing it with new notes. But it is still their song. There is still a center, a core of truth, an eternally burning fire of the faith that has been at the heart of the church's life and the foundation of its belief for two thousand years, which the free churches not only accept but treasure as their own.

Every experience of life contributes to a man's faith. Every moment of insight, every feeling of love, every singing of hope is preparing in his heart the "way of the Lord." And whether it comes through the long years or whether it comes in a Damascus noonday as it came to Paul, it is an experience of trusting, of putting your life into another's hands, and claiming him for your own. Faith is something which, for every man, grows. From the day of its birth until it blossoms and blooms in the years of maturity into the deepest convictions of his soul, it grows within.

And the one to whom Christians of the gathered churches have always given that trust is Jesus Christ. They and their fathers have said, "Jesus Christ is Lord!" and they have meant, "to him we give everything, all that we are, all that we ever will be." They have belonged to him. Their duty has been to him. Their obedience has been to him, and their love and life have been to him.

Just as Jesus Christ is the one reason for the doctrine of the church among free churchmen, so is he also the one reason for their faith. They have believed that where Christ is, there is the church.

Now, many free churchmen accept and believe with their whole hearts every article of Christian belief. They sing like a great song of faith the words of the Apostle's Creed. But they do not ask this of new church members. They do not ask it because they do not find Christ in the New Testament asking it. They ask only that the new Christian be able to say for his life, "Christ is the Saviour of my life, my Lord, and him will I follow!"

It is the following that counts, the growing and increasing in faith that counts.

But who is this Christ in whom the gathered churches believe? We believe he is the Son of God: that in a strange and unique way God came, on a star-filled night in Bethlehem, into the world in the life of a tiny child; that God chose that child to be the instrument of his salvation in the world; that into that tiny life the God of heaven and earth poured himself, so that men might know him as a man, might be close to him, and recognize him, and learn at last to love him. "For God so loved the world, that he gave his only begotten Son, that whosoever believeth in him should not perish, but have everlasting life."

Our belief about this strange event, and about this man who was more than a man, is what the Christian church has called "Trinitarian" belief. We believe—with the whole church—that the one God of the universe has made himself known to men in three Persons—three ways.

From the apostle's point of view, here was the mighty ruler of the world, the God of their fathers and their God, whom they had worshiped ever since the days of Abraham. Peter, and James, and John knew that God and worshiped him on the Sabbath day.

But the children of Israel, through all those years, had repeatedly turned away from their God, until God resolved in his heart to go to his people in a new way, an unmistakable way, a way in which they could recognize him and love him.

Israel had always thought he might do this. The prophets foretold it. A Messiah would come. One day a man stood before two brother-fishermen saying simply, "Follow me." And they followed. And as they lived, and worked, and walked with this man, they sensed an authority about him—"This man speaks as one with authority, and not as the scribes." They began to feel that when he looked at them the eyes of God were looking at them, and that when he spoke to them, God himself was speaking to them. Then one day, when Jesus asked them, "Whom do men say that I . . . am?" Peter answered, "Thou art the Christ, the Son of the Living God!"

All their hope was pinned on him: their hope for Israel, their hope for themselves. Until one day the hammer of history nailed their Saviour to a cross, and he died, and the darkness came in, and the dream was ended. They who had touched the hem of God's garment would never see him again.

—Until on the first day of the week Mary Magdalene came running from the tomb with her wild tale. Until two disciples on their way to Emmaus found the Lord in the breaking of bread. Until he himself came into their upper room—though the door was locked and bolted.

Gradually it dawned upon them what had happened in history—in *their* history. God the Lord had come into their world in a man. In Jesus. He had come in love. Love great enough to die for them "while they were yet sinners." For *all* of them, sinners though they were, this Christ had died, and had marvelously paid with his own life blood the price of their sin. For them and for the world, he had done it. He had paid the bail, he had set them free.

And as for him, he lived. That was the plain fact of it. He lived, and he promised to send them his Spirit—to be with them in a wonderful new way. He ascended into heaven, and told them to wait, and on the day of Pentecost—with tongues of fire and the rushing of a mighty wind from heaven—the Spirit came, the Holy Spirit, the Spirit we know today. It is the Spirit that meets Christian people and moves them in their worship each Sunday. It is the Spirit that guides and leads them in their work and witness every day.

Those men of Galilee knew God the Father. They never ceased to believe in him. But they found him in a new way in the man Christ Jesus. And when he died, they found him yet again, alive and risen—the Holy Spirit, invisible yet powerful, of the same God they had always known.

They saw no conflict in this. It was no theological dilemma for them. It was the experience of their heart.

The doctrine of the Trinity was the later attempt of theologians to put into writing an experience of man that could not be contained in words. It is a stumbling human attempt to describe what is divine and supernatural.

But it is this God, who so loved the world as to come among men in the man Christ Jesus, and to dwell in their hearts today by the Holy Spirit, who is the God in whom the people of the free churches have believed.

It is this essence of the faith, this core of the Christian conviction that has been and is now professed by the church catholic and protestant, orthodox and reformed. It is for the believing of this faith together, expressed through the means of covenant-love, that the gathered church would presume to offer these elements of a true faith to the whole church.

4

The Gathered Church and the Meaning of Ministry

It seems somehow peculiarly ironic that the stumbling block beneath all other stumbling blocks in the search for Christian unity should be the problem of the ministry: the problem of these men, so devoted, so willing to be servants of God and servants of men, and yet possessed of such pride, such pleasure in prerogative, such unseemly interest in their own position.

Loud is the talk today of recovering the place of the laity, of restoring to them their ancient honor, of recovering the true sense of the "priesthood of all believers." And yet the one group within the church most consistently standing in the way of lay leadership and of Christian unity is the professional, ordained ministry. And their reason for concern is the problem of their position. Will they be essential to the church's life in the future, or will they be only one part of the church's life among many? Will they forfeit their privileges and prerogatives in favor of a broader, more inclusive ministry of the whole people, or will they cling to what they have until the tides of the time and the impatience of the people rise up to wrest it from them?

These are stark, disturbing questions within the church today, and yet they are largely unspoken, almost unconscious. Not many ministers are consciously wrestling with the question of doing away with the ordained ministry in favor of a broader, more general ministry of the whole people. Rather, they are conceiving ways in which the office of the minister can be even more securely entrenched in the organization of the church, more universally recognized, and more unquestioningly accepted. Two opposite movements are at work within the church's life, each moving in a different direction. For while the great institutional organizations of the church and the commissions on church unity are accepting principles that will solidify the ministry's position, out on the fringes, and especially in the seminaries, among students and younger faculty, serious questions are being persistently raised about ministry: about whose task it is, about who should fullfill it, and most threatening of all, does ordination have meaning, and is it really necessary at all?

The leaders of denominations, as they explore the possibilities of bishops for the whole church, seem blithely ignorant of the implications of their younger colleagues' questions, and the younger colleagues themselves seem unaware of the implications of their own questions for the problem of ministry in the ecumenical negotiations ahead. The old men say: "Let us take back bishops and their authority in all the churches," and the Young Turks say, "Why do we ordain men to the ministry anyway? What is the point? It is the people who should minister!"

The deeper implication, of course, for the church's life within, centers in the question of the sacraments. How can a nonepiscopally ordained minister possibly administer the Lord's Supper if the church restores the office of the bishop and his powers to ordain, and who would administer the sacraments if there are no ordained clergy?

Interesting dilemma. And a deep dilemma. For the wounds in this area of the church's life are deep—at least for those Protestant churches that three hundred years ago protested the power and prerogatives of the bishop, from the bishop of Rome to the most insignificant bishop of the provinces, and demanded a Reformation that would do away with that office and its temptations. How easy the pose of self-righteousness has been when those of the episcopate charged free church pastors with being no ministers at all, and raised private doubts about the marriages performed, and the sacraments administered, and indeed about the whole pastoral ministry of those whose orders were called in question.

Each has his own stories, his remembrances that rankle. One remembers the man from a free church ministry who felt called to enter an episcopal ministry, until, after due preparation, and study, and examination, he was presented to the bishop who insisted, "You must be rebaptized and profess that you are now becoming a Christian." "But I have been a Christian since childhood," the man replied, "and a Protestant minister too." But the bishop was adamant, and he lost a priest for his church that day. "I cannot deny the faith I've had," was the honest answer that he received.

Or there is the experience of a Protestant minister at an ecumenical youth camp in Connecticut, where a communion service was to be held for all the students on a Sunday morning, only to be destroyed when the bishop of the diocese arrived to insist that his young people could not take part unless he himself were the celebrant of the service.

Or again, in a California college a well-known Methodist minister submitted to Episcopal ordination so that he might minister on the campus to students of that tradition.

Nor can it be very easy on the other side, when millions of Protestants seem to deny the validity of the episcopal office which others treasure and revere, and apparently are saying that they can get along without it, thank you all the same!

A sticky subject indeed, for the wounds of the past still hurt and are sore.

And yet we do live in a day of hope. There are signs of a new understanding, a new openness, and a new appreciation for the validity of both traditions—a new willingness to recognize that God has greatly used both traditions for good and for Christ's glory. In New York City a Roman Catholic monk shared with an Episcopal priest in the performance of a Christian marriage service. In Tamworth, New Hampshire, for ten years an ecumenical ministry has been carried on by an Episcopal minister to three congregations banded together as an "Association": one Baptist, one Congregational, and one Episcopalian. The new respect is real. And the hope of some rapprochement seems real.

But the question still, which will not go away in spite of the new respect and good feeling, is: Can the ordination of Protestant ministers stand? Can Episcopal and free church ordination and ministry be mutually respected and accepted as valid? It is the question facing the ecumenical church to which the churches of the gathered tradition would dare to propose a solution.

The Witness of One Man's Life

But take first of all the rather remarkable example of one man's life. The man was John XXIII, for four and a half years Pope of the Roman Catholic church. The world grieved when he died, and we grieved, too. And that would seem a little odd, because we are not Roman Catholics. But many who were not Roman Catholics grieved. Why? Why should it be?

The reason is that we came to love him. And I know that I came to love him because I found him saying and being something which I myself should in some ways like to say and be:

things which, I believe, we all should want, and which the Christian church needs terribly today.

It would seem all too obvious to say we found ourselves loving him because of something that he was. But it is important to say that because it is important to notice that we did not love him because he was the Pope, or because he had been properly and episcopally ordained. We loved him because of a quality of life, a power of Spirit, a kind of compassion which he had.

John XXIII was, of all things, a pastor. People loved him because they knew that he loved them. The passages from his diary published in *Osservatore Romano* just after his death are a delight, when he wrote such things as: "O, the people of Rome—how I love them!" So simple. So personal. And at the very end of his life, he spoke a special blessing for the people of Rome. Because, as he established very early, he was the bishop of Rome and he made every effort to recover his role as pastor of those people and parishes of the eternal city. Before his death he had actually visited over half of those parishes in person. And I am deeply convinced that his very yearning for unity was because he was a pastor. He just couldn't bear to see men and women all across the world loving the same Lord and yet not loving each other. This simple man was led into a love and concern for other people which the rigid rules and traditions of his church would never normally have encouraged him to feel. But he felt it because he was first of all a pastor who loved people.

Other popes can be recalled in recent memory, but none were like this one. Now, of course, he was a simple man, a man from peasant stock, one of the people. But he really had something which neither his background and upbringing nor his office as Pope had given him. He had something which God had given him: a gift of grace, a gift of the Spirit.

Does not this go to the heart of the quest for unity today? For here is something that can leap across the man-made barriers between Christians and touch them with the God-made bonds that bind us together.

The free churches, the churches of the gathered tradition would propose that this Spirit—this Holy Spirit—is the key to opening the dilemma and dimensions of the ministry.

The Gift of the Spirit: The Key to the Ministry

It is remarkable how little any idea of the Holy Spirit enters into modern discussion of the nature of the ministry. Those who question both the validity and relevance of ordination do so because they can see nothing that distinguishes a minister from the layman. If both are called to minister why should one be set apart in a special way that the other is not? On the other side are the defenders of the *status quo* among the liturgical and episcopally organized denominations defending a form of the ministry purely on the basis of a presumed physical continuance over many years, and on the following of a particular form of ordination to that ministry—neither of them proposing anything more than purely functional or physical reasons for defending their view of the ministry.

Surely both are missing the point. Even psychologically they are missing the point. They conform to nothing the world knows about the ministry, and to nothing the much-discussed but poorly understood laity know about the ministry.

Ask any of them about any minister and they will answer you what many of them answer about Pope John—or Billy Graham, or Peter Marshall, or their own minister. They will say: "He is a good man," or "He is my friend and I love him," or "He is a great preacher who helped me find Christ." Or they will say (and they do about more ministers than we who are ministers like to think) "He is a fraud," or "He is a pompous ass," or "He talks a pretty good game, but he doesn't seem to live it!"

This is what the laity care about; whether the man who is

a minister "is for real." They want him to be for real, they want him to be the real article because they hold innately a high view of the ministry—higher than do many ministers themselves. Oddly enough, they seem to want the minister to be a man of God. They curiously want him to be a holy man, a man who knows God, who walks with God, a man of prayer, a man of faith, and a man therefore of some real power.

But in the ministry today it is not very fashionable to be a holy man, a man of devotion and prayer, a man who has the hand of the Lord upon his heart. The cry instead is to be "relevant," to be a man well acquainted with the secular city, a man who knows the "spots," and who knows the people who make the city hum. They would point out that Jesus was all these things. But they forget that he was a man of God in the secular city, and in the company of prostitutes, and in the homes of tax collectors.

Any examination of the New Testament reveals, however, that the one gift essential to ministry was the gift of the Holy Spirit. The whole point of Pentecost was that, for all their training and education in the company of Jesus himself, for all their knowledge of the truth about Christ, the disciples and their new young church would not be finally ready to fulfill their ministry until they had received the gift of the Spirit; "until ye be endued with power from on high."

The ministry's power is spiritual power, and that power is given when the gift of God's Spirit, God's love, God's abiding presence in Christ is given. The New Testament attests this again and again. Paul comes upon a group of Christians and says, "Have you received the Holy Spirit since you believed?" and when they admit they have not he bids them kneel, lays his hands upon them, prays, and the gift is given. Stephen's ministry was obviously characterized as a ministry of the Spirit.

The point here is that by their very life as churches the gathered church has remembered this. The gathered churches by their whole way of life have cast themselves upon God's

Spirit. With their belief that "where two or three are gathered together in my name, there am I in the midst of them," they have made their whole witness dependent upon the Spirit. On the grounds that where two or three met faithfully together Christ would be with them in the midst, the earliest Congregationalists defied the Church in England and set up, in houses and barns, what they believed, according to the New Testament model, to be true churches of Jesus Christ. Their reasoning was that Christ's presence—his Spirit—in their midst was what made them truly and fully the church. Therefore, their whole enterprise was staked upon the powerful presence of the Spirit. Surely, then, the ministry too was dependent upon and validated by the presence and powerful working of that same Spirit.

If a man did not "have the Spirit" then he was not of Christ. And if that same Spirit is not present in such a church's worship and life, then it is no true church. The Spirit has been, for the gathered churches, their reason for being and the only authentication of their being. The whole purpose for being free from ecclesiastical control, and from creeds and confessions, has been so that they could be absolutely free to follow the leading of the living Lord. If he is truly alive, they have reasoned, then he can indeed rule the church, he can guide and direct and exercise authority over the church—over each local, gathered church, just as he promised.

This is the quality that has characterized the churches at the left end of Protestantism: they have depended upon the Spirit. They have organized their life so that they could be flexible, free to respond to the leadings of the Spirit. And at their best they have learned that the Spirit "moves where it listeth," that it cannot be organized or controlled. They have learned that they must be ready for invasions of this supernatural power from without. This is why worship is so unstructured in some traditions, so open to sudden change, and why anyone in that company may expect to be caught up by the sweeping power of the Spirit and called upon to speak and give witness and testimony.

Much more staid has been the worship of others and yet both of these traditions have learned to conceive their "way" as an open way, a pilgrim way, a way of Christian life that is ready at a moment's notice to pack up and move out in new directions and on new missions.

Obviously, such traditions depend upon ministries of the Spirit: upon ministers who are themselves attuned to the mind and working of the Spirit, who are able to open up the Spirit's way in their people's heart.

No such ministry, therefore, just as no such church, could depend on a form forged in law, and protocol, and physical inheritance—whether from father to son or from bishop to bishop.

The Ministry a High and Holy Thing

In such a tradition, then, the ministry is thrust back from the area of the mechanical and intellectual, into the realm of the divine and the spiritual. This is not to say that "spiritual" is without "intellectual" or that the Divine does not use earthly means, but rather to say that to anything which, in another tradition, may have been viewed as in any way automatic or mechanical, or even traditional (as ordination might be conceived), there is here added an almost numinous quality, a quality of the *"mysterium tremendum"* of God's unpredictable Spirit, a quality which may well add dimensions of charisma, the special spiritual quality of leadership, to the man involved.

For all their free church lack of form and pageantry in worship, and their lack of clerical collars and crosses in street dress, the churches of the gathered tradition have held the ministry to be a high and holy thing. Too high, in fact, to be connected with such mechanical or symbolic things as clerical dress or customs of preferment.

The fact that the free churches have had no bishop nor any Presbytery has never meant that entrance into the ministry was a thing lightly taken. Personally, I have found nothing so awesome nor so significant as an ordination or an installation service in a church of the gathered tradition. It is significant because—far from lining up a whole crew of men to be ordained all at once—it is personal. Every word is directed to that young man and the ministry he is about to undertake, and to that congregation who have called him to be their own. Pastor and people are tied inextricably together, for almost always it is in the actual church he is going to serve that a man is ordained, and certainly in which he is installed. This is rather a different thing from ordination in the diocesan cathedral along with a whole "class" of men.

It is made even more personal because earlier in the day, or within two or three weeks, a rather rigorous public examination has been conducted, at which the young man stated his faith and gave reason for the convictions that were in him, and was then closely questioned. The whole experience partakes of qualities as diverse as Ph.D. oral exams, graduation exercises, and marriage vows.

And when the one man kneels, and the hands of the people and of his "fathers and brethren" in the ministry are placed upon his head and he is ordained by the heartfelt joining of their prayers for him—especially the prayer that the Holy Spirit in all its fullness might be granted him—well then, you have the makings not only of high drama, but of deep devotion and commitment: a moment which the living Christ can use in marvelous ways!

It is the conviction in the gathered church that something happens in an ordination service. The free church view of the ministry is a "high" view, a view that something divine as well as human is taking place in that service of worship, just as they believe something divine is taking place in every service of worship.

This is the moment of personal, public commitment. This is the moment when a young man or woman, for the first time, publicly acknowledges the call he has received from his Lord, and responds to it. It does not mean that the call comes in that moment, nor that he is just then responding to it. Long before, the call may have come, and in his heart he may long since have responded to it, but never publicly, never before the world. The transaction is like the transaction of marriage: the final public promise, the vow before God and the world which must now be kept. At any point along the way, just as in engagement, he might have turned back, but now no longer. It is a promise of life, a dedication of self.

Let no man say ordination to the ministry is meaningless! Only lack of an honest faith on the part of the ordained could make it that. It is the setting aside, by the people of God, of a man whom God has chosen and whom they have chosen, to be their pastor and teacher in a way that none of them can be. They may have great gifts of spirit, and life, and understanding. But their ministry is in the world. They are called to minister in the office, on the assembly line, and in the market place. Their ministry is real, and it is total. But it is different. And their ministries depend upon his ministry. The man they ordain to be a minister is being set aside by God's people to be their teacher and their pastor. If they are to fulfill their ministries, they will need his ministry—his ministry of regularly and faithfully expounding to them the Scriptures, of teaching and helping them to grow in faith, and of ministering to them in their own times of darkness and sorrow.

He is not the church! Make no mistake about that. In the free church view he is not conceived of as essential for making them truly the church. A gathered church is fully and completely the church because it is gathered around Christ and has been gathered by Christ. As long as they gather in Christ's name, believing in him, witnessing to him, and seeking his help—then Christ is there, in his Spirit, and his presence is all that is needed to make them fully and truly the church. The ordained ministry is that most important ministry of apostleship, of prophecy, of teaching, of pastoring which Paul named as pre-eminent. The people are called to equally valid ministries of a different nature.

But because their ministries, in the long run, depend so much on his ministry, and because it is crucial that they be not led astray, but be nurtured and taught and raised up faithfully in the Faith, it is crucial that the ordained minister, as their apostle, prophet, and teacher, be a man of the Spirit, a man in whom and upon whom the Spirit dwells, a man who is not only well trained and educated, and a person of character and integrity, but a man gripped by the Holy Spirit.

It is, therefore, that ordination is conceived among the free churches as not only recognizing the young man's personal gifts from God, and his call from God, and the church's own call to him, but also as that service of worship, that particular time and place in history when they, as God's people in that place, fully representing the whole Church of Christ, beseech with all their faith and power the one final gift from God that will give life and power to this young man's abilities, that will set him aflame not only with faith but with all those other special qualities of grace that can make him truly a man of God, a man in Christ. That is, the gift of the Holy Spirit: the gift which the church received at Pentecost, the gift which Stephen and Paul received, the gift which the whole church must receive afresh again and again if it is to be truly the church.

The gift of the Spirit is the key to the ministry.

The Holy Spirit and the Apostolic Ministry

Is this emphasis upon the place of the Spirit a sufficient claim to make for the validity of the gathered church's ministry alongside that of the episcopal traditions of the Roman Catholic, Episcopalian, and Methodist churches? The witness of the New Testament and the first-century church's life would indicate that it is.

Jesus' own concern was for the faith of his disciples, that they know him and the God who had sent him, that they know the message of his death, and Resurrection, and living power to tell the world, and that they receive the Spirit to be their comforter and guide and power. There is no record of any formal classification of his men by Jesus, except that they were all disciples, learners, preparing for a great ministry after his death and Resurrection. They were set aside, evidently, as a group, from the much larger number of those who followed Jesus, who were also disciples and followers. They were apparently set aside for special training and preparation so that they could give total time to the ministry, just as the professional ministry is set aside today. The apostolic ministry in the early church, while it began as an itinerant, evangelical, and missionary ministry as in the case of Peter, and Paul, and Philip, became very soon a pastoral ministry as with Timothy and James.

The one crucial concern in that first-century church was the message, and the Christ who was the subject and the living proof of the message. Every letter of Paul is concerned not with who is a minister according to proper ordination or ecclesiastical claim, but rather with whether the gospel, the truth of Christ is being faithfully proclaimed and lived.

It is the claim of the free churches that the "apostolic succession" is most truly inherited and passed on where there is obedience to the apostolic gospel rather than a claim to be a visible line of intact succession through episcopal ordinations.

That the line of succession to Peter as the first bishop of Rome is historically questionable has not seemed sufficiently important to be the primary argument of the free churches. It has seemed to them that far more important in laying claim to being successors of the apostles is the evidence of the spiritual realities of being true to Christ himself. That the Church of Rome in Reformation days violated that trust and betrayed the Spirit would seem sufficient proof that the "apostolic succession" in any really relevant and meaningful terms was broken then. It has been broken since, to be sure, by churches and ministers in the free church tradition. But wherever the ministry of the church has been such that Christ's Spirit was able to use it as an instrument for the reconciling and restoring of men, there has been the "apostolic succession."

The "succession" which counts is not the succession of office but the "succession" of faith in the gospel. A booklet published in London in 1953 makes the point well when it asks: "Does T. W. Manson bring us even closer to the true answer when he tells us that what binds the church of today to the church of apostolic times is not the continuance in it of a valid ministry but the continuance of the ministry of the Risen Christ?"[1] The claim of the gathered church is that it is Christ himself who is the basis both of the unity and the continuity of the church.

But no emphasis upon the Spirit is meant to deny the need for standards in the ministry. The gathered churches by tradition have claimed high standards for the ministry, even while valuing the usually much less definable qualities of the Spirit. Education of the ministry has been a primary principle. Colleges have been founded by concerned Christians for the express purpose of carrying on an educated ministry. Ordination has long required high standards of education, in the belief that the background in education coupled with the

[1] *Congregational Churchmanship*, p. 17, published by Congregational Council, London, England.

experience of a call from God and a personal decision to serve would provide all the preparation the church could provide for the giving of the Holy Spirit in God's good time.

It is the Spirit in the end which gives to the church an apostolic ministry.

The Ministry of the People

Part of the Protestant claim for its own understanding of "apostolic succession" is its doctrine of the priesthood of all believers. By God's grace every Christian man has direct access to the heavenly Father through Christ and may be a minister of that grace to his brother.

Humbly and hopefully the gathered church would offer to the great church a form of life and witness that has sought faithfully to preserve that ministry of the people. All across the church the cry has gone up that the layman's place must be recognized again. Even the Roman Catholic Church is taking steps to demonstrate this in its life and worship, with a layman stationed in the altar area, and reading the Scriptures to the people.

And yet here in the life of the gathered churches the place of the layman has at least been meant to be supreme. It is his church. His to fashion, his to direct, his to love and lead and lift high, if he will. His also to fail. And the difference between success and failure has been between that church having Christ as its heart, or not having Christ.

And there is no free churchman with any honesty at all who could not document the frequent failure of free churches to live up to this ideal. Because the free churches are more open in their freedom than most, the selfishness of men and the power of the devil himself have their opportunity to work. Indeed, this is precisely why the more authoritarian church traditions have refused to run the risk of such freedom.

A gathered church can be a great temptation to a layman

who little understands his faith and heritage and who wants to run his church the way he runs his business, without any sense of openness to the leading of the Holy Spirit. And some free churches, even under the guise of being a "church for the laymen," have been sinfully dominated by ministers who have fashioned the church they served in their own image.

But this is because they have abused the gift of freedom and because they have not submitted themselves in obedience to Christ's leading and Lordship, which is the commitment they made when they chose the free church way. The gathered churches offer no safe harbor from sin and human error. But they do provide a form of life which gives men a chance to follow their Lord in a humble and dignified way that gives every man a place of importance in the life of the church.

It is in the gathered church that Christ is meant directly to rule. It is their conviction that he speaks not so much through a denominational office, or a bishop's hand, or a Presbytery's ruling, as directly to the people themselves, who are the church. Church government, in the gathered church, demands that the people meet regularly together to attend to their business, to share their great concerns. And it is there, as they meet in the spirit of prayer and openness, that Christ can come directly among the two or three gathered together, to lead them, to make his will known, to exercise his authority over them.

That authority is not exercised by speaking some divine obscure word to the minister alone for him to pass on to the people. It is spoken to the people themselves—perhaps first to the littlest, least significant, out-of-the-way person there. As he stands up to speak his concern, other minds and hearts will be caught up, and soon the whole meeting will sense the movement of the Spirit in their midst as they seem, inevitably, to be led toward one common decision. No executive committee, no session, or wardens, or council, or bishop has given them directive. Not even their own minister has given them directive. Christ has given them his directive. He has gone directly to the people. I can think of nothing to exalt the laity more than that.

But what are the implications of this? The gathered church is the people's church. Under the leading of Christ they may make their decisions, and determine their future. They may call their own minister. And they may ordain and install him.

If they are the church by virtue of being the two or three gathered together with Christ in the midst, then all power falls to them. And they are called, under Christ, to exercise it. In ordination the whole church prays for the giving of the Spirit. The whole church—through its deacons or other representatives—lays hands sometimes (along with brother ministers of the region) upon the young man to be ordained. The whole church ordains to the ministry. It is the people's ministry, their high and holy task.

In the gathered church the minister is usually not even the moderator of the "meeting" that makes the vital decisions. The minister becomes a member of the church he serves as a sign of his own place as one of the people. Any authority he has under Christ is given to him as a minister in that place by the call of the people whom Christ has gathered and given authority.

The genius of the gathered church as a way of church life is that it offers the great church a concept of ministry which includes a high and apostolic view of the ordained ministry while at the same time honoring, and exalting, and ultimately depending upon the ministry of the lay people.

No view of apostolic succession, of clerical ordination through a physical line of bishops can ever give back to the layman the rightful place he once held in the earliest days of the church's life. Inevitably, in both Roman Catholic and Episcopal churches, this sets the clergy apart, if not as a higher order of being, then at least as officers with highest authority in the church's life. The only way the layman can ever share in that authority is to become a clergyman, to be ordained into the physical succession.

But if, on the contrary, that apostolic succession is one of faith, then all the people, when they share that faith, share not only the apostolic succession but also its authority. Ordination is no longer done by agreement between seminary and ecclesiastical officials. It is done by the people themselves, voluntarily, gladly, for the express purpose of fulfilling a ministry which they have called a man to fulfill.

The ordained ministry is vital and necessary. But it is exercised by the express calling of the people. Nor does it, once given, exalt a minister above his people. For his only power, his only honor, his only right to love, and affection, and "place" among his people is his only by virtue of the love and concern and power granted to him by gift of the Holy Spirit. His authority is not of office, but is of the man he becomes by the gift of the Spirit and the love of his people.

The people's ministry is left to be as full as they can make it—indeed, as full as their Lord and as their minister can help them to make it. For the peculiar purpose of the pastor's ministry is to so teach, and preach, and lead, and lift up that the people will be set free to fulfill their ministry. And it is that ministry which will be the peculiar and lasting ministry of that congregation. Their ministry is to believe the gospel, to pray for the sick, the weary, and the world, to witness to their Lord wherever they are, and to serve their Christ in the world in those peculiar and strategic places Christ puts them—from the president's office in a great company to the school teacher's classroom in a country school house. Their ministry is Christ's ministry, the ministry of the Spirit—

> ... to preach the gospel to the poor; ... to heal the brokenhearted, to preach deliverance to the captives, and recovering of sight to the blind, to set at liberty those that are bruised. To preach the acceptable year of the Lord.

There is no minister faithful to his calling who has not seen Christ raise up among his own people powerful spirits who ministered in ways he knew he never could: men and women great in faith, great in prayer, great in the Spirit; men and women obviously chosen by Christ as his servants and soldiers without benefit of apostolic succession or the rest.

The Spirit is the key to the people's ministry, and their ministry is the key to power and renewal in the whole church. They are the gift that the gathered church would give. It offers an apostolic succession of faith, a valid ministry by test of the Spirit, and a people's place essential for them in the life of a Spirit-church.

The ministry of such a church must be a Spirit ministry, a ministry of love and care and proclamation given by God's Holy Spirit. It is a ministry centering among people, where they are gathered together in worship and work and witness. A minister is one who ministers—who preaches the gospel, who teaches the Word, who serves the sacraments, who prays for people, who goes into all the world according to Christ's command. But the name of minister in the free church tradition belongs to those of the gathered church, those who are its people, and those who serve its people.

What the gathered churches offer the whole church, then, is a ministry centered in that level of church life which all denominations share: the congregation. It offers a view of the church and the ministry which exalts the congregation and its ministers, both lay and clerical. It takes nothing from any other denomination's "way," it simply opens up depths of meaning at the heart of *every* denomination's "way." It points, in fact, to an acceptance of the valid ministries of every church, by making the test of all, the Spirit. And it is in keeping, free churchmen believe, with the ministry of One who, long. ago, taught us that the Spirit always is the valid test.

Such would the gathered church contribute to the meaning of the ministry in this day of ecumenical concern.

5

The Gathered Church and God's People at Worship

In the life of the Christian church nothing is more important, in any age or at any time, than the life of its people at worship. If the church is irrelevant and meaningless here, it will be irrelevant and meaningless in the world. If it is exciting and victorious here, it will be exciting and victorious in the world. Charge the church to be active and influential in social causes, yes. Spur it on to activity in every area of life, by all means. But neglect its mission and its ministry here, and it will die. It will be a dead institution with nothing to say anywhere to anyone.

For all across the world, wherever you find the church, worship is the heart of it. Worship is where it all begins. Worship is where the community of the faithful offers itself to God—where it receives the instructions for its work in the world, and where the concerns of the world are brought before God. And if the church of Christ today is ever to be reformed or renewed, if it is ever to rise up from the valley of the dry bones and live, it will have to do it first here, in public worship.

God's People at Worship

The Trouble with the Church

We live in a day of great dissatisfaction with the church. The apathy without is obvious. In England the church estimates that fewer than 10 per cent of all members are now attending public worship. In America the situation is much more deceptive, with booming budgets and awesome edifices, but those who are perceptive at all know that a vast number of the church's members are uncommitted and worship only occasionally. And for those beyond the church it is not taken too seriously—a harmless institution, peopled by a few do-gooders, nothing to worry about, and certainly nothing to get excited about.

To fight the apathy and to get the church moving again, the cry of the critics within the church has been increasingly, "Get the church out on the street, bring it out from behind its fortress walls, and get it into the mainstream of life. Get it into the social revolution of our time. Get it into the movement for racial justice. Make its voice heard in the lobbies in Washington. Get it on record in favor of voting rights, and school desegregation, and urban renewal, and open housing, and poverty legislation, and medical care for the aged—then it will be in the swim, then it will be relevant and significant, then it will make an impact on society, then the world will know its sincerity and good intentions and come flocking to its doors!" The Protestant churches, at least, in America today, are being swept into a program that sees salvation for the church and for the world in largely social, activist terms. Get a good "relevant" program of social change going, the cry goes, and you've got it made!

And a social concern is right. The church must care. The church must do what it can. But that is not the church's primary business. That is not the church's charge from its Lord. That charge is "Go ye into all the world, and preach the gospel . . ." It is "go into all the world and tell men the good news that God loves them. Tell them they are precious in his sight; that he cares about them; that he knows their sin; that he knows how guilty they feel about it, and that he offers a way to save them from their turmoil. Tell them about Christ. Tell them he died the death that was theirs to die; that the debt is paid; that they can be free and unafraid if they'll accept that payment and the one who paid. Tell them that in Christ they have a hope." The Gospel is the heart of it, and worship is the context.

It is interesting indeed that one of the most powerful editorial voices for the church's social concern, the magazine *Renewal*, should have looked long and hard at the sickness of the church and put its finger powerfully and persuasively on the heart of the matter, owning that it is not ultimately the church's failure to be involved with social concerns that repels the world, but something far deeper. Writing in the December, 1963 issue of *Renewal*, Stephen Rose, its editor, says:

> But there is another more widespread manner in which the church repels the world: by being a bore, by sanctimony and self-preening, by cliquishness, by dishonesty, by insipidity, by cleaving to the stereotype of the clergyman as a "soft face over a hard collar," by erecting monuments of stone in order to avoid encounter beyond the institutional fortress.
>
> There is one message that the church needs desperately to hear and understand. It is not simply the church's failures in social action that wrongfully alienates the world. . . . The reason is more profound, more disturbing. The sensitive person rejects the churches when they seem to be social work groups, and no more. The sensitive person rejects the churches when Holy Communion seems more a Hollywood production than a Sacrament, when preaching seems more polished than honest, and when the shared life of the congregation seems to lack authenticity.

And here is the real condemnation:

> There are countless people who despair of the churches not because the church failed to make the right racial pronouncement at the right moment, but because when they attended church in hope, they heard a sermon that they could not respect or sat through a service disrupted by blatant appeals for funds and other inconsequential announcements. . . . The church erects the greatest gulf between itself and the world not because people have an innate hostility to the church but because a desperately seeking people has been so often discouraged by inconsequential preaching and empty worship.[1]

We do not like to admit this. We do not like to think that this is true. But time and time again the worship of the church leaves the world just cold. Time and time again it does not speak to the heart of what the world is hungering to hear.

The Hunger for the Spirit

What the church of Christ and the leaders of the church of Christ must understand is that the world—seeking masses and church members alike—is looking for a quality and not a quantity in the church's worship. It is looking for something intangible, undefined, but nevertheless very real. It is looking for something in the very heart and life of both the preacher and the people who represent the church to them.

There is a great deal of talk these days about "communicating the gospel" as if what is needed is not only new means and media, but also a new language, a new idiom. Unquestionably new words must be found and new meaning put into old words if the eternal Word is to get through to modern men. But what the avant-garde leaders of the church today do not yet understand is that the world is looking to the church not

---

[1] "The Marks of Renewal," by Stephen Rose, *Renewal*, pp. 5-6, December, 1963, Chicago.

nearly so much for new words and a new idiom as it is looking for new men and a new people. For two thousand years it has been the changed life, the new creature, the new man, the man with a faith, the man with the Spirit who has been really convincing, who has really "communicated," who has really convinced and changed other men.

It is this quality of "spirit" with which the world unconsciously, I think, is testing the church today. It is out of patience with the staid forms, the stuffy customs, and the shallow people it has too often found. It wants an end to insincerity and preachy tones and unreal piety.

This is why the great interest in new forms of worship and church life: the small groups, the idea of retreat, store-front churches, worker-priests as in France, coffee shops manned by Christians as in Burlington, Vermont, and Washington, D.C., the Jazz Mass, and the whole relation between religion and drama, religion and painting, religion and poetry.

They are hungry for the Spirit—and they really want to find it in people. A letter came once from a visitor in one congregation:

> Last Sunday as I sat alone in the pew, knowing no one around me, I felt the need to run, and speak to someone. However, when the Deacons began the handshaking (after the communion) it offered me an excellent opportunity, and I turned and spoke to the lady next to me as we were leaving. It seemed the handshake which passed on from one to another did seem to make the atmosphere more friendly.

I cannot believe this is unimportant. Rather, it is crucial in the life of the church: that certain something that one heart can give to another; that quality of the Spirit that can leap over barriers between people which no amount of legal compromising can do.

Oddly enough, the seminaries say nothing about this. They never teach it, they never acknowledge it; do they not really know that the Spirit is the secret of the church's power, the one great hope of the church?

The Gathered Church and the Power of the Spirit

But where can it be found? Where is the Spirit? How can the world know and be filled with this strange power which the prophet Joel promised would be poured out upon all people, and which men of old came to see in the lives of the Johns, and the Pauls, and the Stephens of the first century?

It can be found where men are looking for the Spirit, where they have opened their lives to his guidance, where they are living their common life in such a way that there is freedom for the Spirit, where the Spirit is expected, and where men are absolutely dependent upon him.

Let it be understood here that there is no "way" that owns the Holy Spirit, that can limit him to one tradition, that can claim him for its own. But there are some "ways" that make it harder for him to work, and some that make it easier: some churches expect the Spirit's movement and eagerly, watchfully, wait for him; but others whose life is more narrowly defined and confined fear the unpredictability of the Spirit in their midst, and prefer order, and form, and law.

And primary among those churches where the doors are open and life is free, and where people depend upon and look for the leading of God's Spirit, are the free churches, the gathered churches, the church in which no bishop rules nor hierarchy guides, but where Christ directly and immediately makes his will known to the people themselves who are waiting and hoping that he will come.

Now this is not an arrogant presumption. It is simply a recognition that an independent church, by its very nature, depends utterly upon the Holy Spirit, and derives its essential meaning from its expressed purpose of living with and by the presence of this Spirit in its midst. There is no discipline and no authority except that of Jesus Christ, exercised by the power of his Holy Spirit.

The early fathers of the free church tradition said: "Jesus is Lord." They demanded freedom only to obey him. They threw themselves completely upon him, saying, "Lord, if this is true: if indeed, where two or three are gathered together in thy name thou art there in the midst of them, be in our midst, lead us, be our Guide and God!"

They conceived a whole way of church life—or rather, discovered it in the Bible—based upon this assumption. If Christ made this promise seriously, they reasoned, then his presence amid faithful people is the only thing needed to make a congregation a true church. And they knew that without that, they were nothing—an empty, utter failure as a church: sheer anarchy with no order or authority. But with it they were a conquering host, the church of Christ in fullness and in power!

And the belief of the free churches through the countless years has been that where they were true to that calling as gathered churches in their continuing life, they would be true to that calling also in the great experience of worship.

To those who have looked through liturgical eyes the gathered church way may have seemed too simple and bare. It may even have seemed sloppy and disorganized. But it had an "open end," an open end so that nothing could obscure the way for Christ to come in.

The Gathered Church and Its Gift to Great Worship

All this may seem an affront and an insult, especially to those who love the rich old language, and the symbolic symmetry, and the measured tread of the great liturgical services. But such as the gathered church has it would give gratefully and humbly, and without snobbery or exclusiveness. It would make its gift thoroughly appreciating the values of other traditions, but boldly seeking a hearing for one which has been lost along the way. It offers an open way and a free way, which can include much variety. But it has at least a simple direction and a central purpose, which is to make known the living Lord to longing men.

It has, indeed, the same faults and foibles as other worship. It has all the limitations and temptations among its ministers—especially the temptations to individualism and idiosyncrasy which a free tradition allows. Nor are its people always the most sophisticated. But make not the mistake that Browning made that Christmas night when he condemned the worship of the simple people in their little chapel.

> 'Twas too provoking!
> My gorge rose at the nonsense and stuff of it;
> So, saying like Eve when she plucked
> the apple,
> "I wanted a taste, and now there's enough
> of it,"
> I flung out of the little chapel.

Until . . .

> All at once I looked up with terror.
> He was there.
> He himself with his human air.
> On the narrow pathway, just before,
> I saw the back of him, no more—
> He had left the chapel, then, as I.
> I forgot all about the sky.
> No face: only the sight
> Of a sweepy garment, vast and white,
> With a hem that I could recognize.
> I felt terror, no surprise;
> My mind filled with the cataract,
> At one bound of the mighty fact.
> "I remember, he did say
> Doubtless that, to this world's end,

> Where two or three should meet and pray,
> He would be in the midst, their friend;
> Certainly he was there with them!" [1]

Other forms of worship, too, are spoiled by barriers in the form of men—men in the pulpit as well as the pew. But here in the freedom of an open form many things can happen which, in the whole church, are going to have to happen!

It first of all is the *People's Worship*. The whole tradition and the setting cries it out. The gathered way is the "congregational" way—the way in which the congregation is gathered around Christ in a fellowship formed by his promise to be with them in the midst if they meet as two or three in his name.

The people's very purpose in their coming is to meet this Man directly, this Christ, Who has said he would be there. They come with the cry "Sir, we would see Jesus!" and it is an awesome charge to any man who dares stand up before them! Because it is "congregational" worship it depends upon them. For there is nothing else. In other traditions a beautiful liturgy and set prayers and symbolic motions would save the day and they would leave with something; but this, so free and open, if they bring nothing of themselves it is sure that they will take nothing away.

Because they see the church as gathered around the Lord, it is logical that in the form of worship Christ be conceived to dwell amongst the people. He is there, not in a box upon the altar, and not in the wall behind the same. His place is where the people are, and from Reformation days it has been the custom of the preacher to face his people as a sign of that. In communion he does not serve the supper from before the table with his back to the flock, but facing them from behind the table he serves. He does not normally face a cross as

---

[1] From Robert Browning, "*Christmas Eve and Easter Day.*"

though the Christ were there, but rather acknowledges his place in the people's midst.

Other signs which most traditions share are *the people's songs they sing*. Free church worship is the people's worship, and they are there to sing God's praise. Choirs may come and organ may sound, but it is the people's praise and they must sing it.

And of course, in some traditions of the gathered churches the music is just taken over by the congregation. They find a beat and hum and sing. The Spirit moves and they move, too. And so have come to America the Negro spirituals, her only authentic, native music.

But it is *in prayer as well, the people's place is seen*. For the great heritage of the gathered church, the free church, is free prayer. This is prayer which the people share. In some traditions they share aloud, but even among the more formal traditions, where not a word is said, the people pray. They pray on entering the church, as every Christian should, but they pray too in the pastor's prayer which really is the people's prayer. It is the people's prayer because it is prayed for them, and more truly still, by them. The preacher is only the mouth, the voice, to express the high praise, the deep longings, and the petitions of the people.

It is no set prayer, beautiful but old, generalized to meet all conditions and said from generation to generation through the church's years. It is as fresh as the new day and up to date as the morning paper, and it speaks the people's heart and life— or so it hopes to do.

But people of the gathered church came together to meet their Lord. That is why some churches in old New England are still called "meeting houses." And that meeting is done especially, through God's Word to men, and hence the *preaching gift* by a man to men.

He speaks in Scripture, too, and that is faithfully read in every service, and then expounded in a sermon—a message from that "Word" in Scripture to the Word of God in human hearts. So the preacher is the proclaimer of that precious Word, and the Word is valued, and looked for so the people hold it aloft—high and lifted up—in a pulpit mighty as a throne, where the cry of the King of kings can be heard. And the people symbolically are gathered around that Word, around that pulpit so the Bible and its place of prominence would be in their midst, the better for them to hear.

And with the pulpit comes *the table—the free table,* in a grand tradition, *meant for friends.* For in the gathered church the sacraments are served, and the Lord's Supper of all is the most precious. To the free church fathers, the Scriptures seemed to say this sacrament was a supper, not a sacrifice. And so, what to some is still an altar is to them a table—a table at which a dozen men could sit and eat. So in the gathered church it is conceived that the people, wherever they sit, are gathered around the table. It is their central symbol along with the pulpit, for from both is the bread of life broken open for them—from the pulpit is the Word spoken, and from the table is the Word acted out.

Behind the table the minister stands and faces the people. And because it is Christ's table at which he serves it is to all whom Christ would call that he extends the great invitation: "Come unto me, all ye . . . !" Nor is it grace cheaply given, for the table is not ours but Christ's to set, and he may welcome whom he will. Far be it from us to exclude any man who understands what he is doing and takes it in that spirit. At an Episcopal, or Lutheran, or Roman table free churchmen may not be welcome, but in the meeting houses of the gathered people the way is clear and the table is free for Christ to call whom he will.

This surely is not said to point in self-righteous pride to the gathered church's tolerance, to say, "Look how free and generous we are, and you so stingy and selfish." It is to say rather that if there is ever to be a unity in the church—whatever its form—it must be where mutual ministries are recognized, and where common sacraments are shared. It is to say that unless we can make a break-through at the Lord's table we are unlikely to make a break-through anywhere.

The furor within Catholicism at the rebaptism of a president's daughter has dramatized to the world the very sensitive concern of that church to preserve the one ecumenical sacrament which they share with the rest of Christ's church, the sacrament of baptism. The president's daughter had been baptized originally by an Episcopal priest in the name of the Father, the Son, and the Holy Ghost and therefore, according to many Catholics, her original baptism should have sufficed—even though she was entering the Catholic church. The Catholic church does not require baptism to be performed necessarily by an ordained priest.

Perhaps we have gravely sinned as churches to have thrown up such a barrier around the even more common sacramental experience, the sharing of the Lord's Supper. Is it really, after all, a man's proper ordination that makes him worthy to minister to God's people either in Word or Sacrament? Much rather, it is the presence of the Holy Spirit in his life and in the midst of the people whom Christ has gathered together to eat at his table.

The principle of unity is the principle of the Spirit, then, the Holy Spirit, the Spirit of Christ, and his true presence among the people, and not the principle of proper mechanical ordination.

It is for this principle that the free churches would stand. Their testimony, as the whole church seeks a break-through to a common table for all Christians, is that our looking for and accepting the Spirit of Christ in a man's ministry and in a gathered church's life is the one legitimate test and standard for common access for all Christians of every denomination to the one free table of our Lord.

We must accept that it is his table and not ours. We only

set it for him. We only act for him. And when we act for him we must act in his Spirit, which is the Spirit of acceptance, of welcoming home, of letting the little children come unto him. Our sin is in placing the barrier, not in welcoming too freely.

The challenge to the whole church, then, is to believe the Spirit—really to trust Christ to rule, to draw all men unto him, to do in fact what he has promised to do. The challenge to the whole church, really, is to trust, to believe, to accept Christ and to act in the Spirit he manifested and in the Spirit in which it was evidently possible for the first-century church to act. And its one question—always—was: "Have ye received the Spirit since ye believed?"

As Spirit churches, welcoming all who come in the Spirit, a new way can be found for a new day of common communion for all Christians: a day when we can sit down, Catholic, Episcopalian, Congregationalist, Presbyterian, Baptist, and Pentecostalist alike, at a table set for friends, by Christ.

In any church that remembers a Christ who calls even little children unto him, the gathered church makes *baptism as a sacrament central*, too.

Through all the long heritage of the free churches both sacraments were conceived as central to the whole people's life. Just as communion was rarely given to private persons except as extensions of the common meal, so baptism is the congregation's rite and is no service for private chapel or family home.

It is a sacrament for all the people, and in the gathered church the people share it. Deacons often lead in this service too, and the whole church participates.

In worship as in all our life the church is seen as the people's church—theirs to pray and sing and bear up in love, but also theirs to lead and point the way. The minister preaches and may lead in prayer, but it is the people's prayers that keep him there. They pray for him and for the world. They too can preach and pray, and on occasion do. It is the privilege of deacons to baptize and serve the supper if the church, seeking Christ's leading, so requires.

As in the "meeting" where under Christ's direct authority the church is governed, it is the people and not the preacher whose church it is, and who bear the burden. The meeting itself a layman leads, and were no preacher present, worship too he would lead. For over two years the Pilgrims at Plymouth were led by a layman, William Brewster, their elder. The pastor they loved never came, but he taught them well, and they lived on those teachings, and their Lord's special leadings.

Renewal and Reform

The exciting thing in such a day as this is that suddenly by the winds of the Spirit the whole church now is stirring and a new day has come. Across the whole church it has come. The word is everywhere of what even the Vatican Council seeks. The stirrings have been to the depths, and into a world of primarily Protestant ecumenicity—ecumenicity that was getting a little tired, at last burst suddenly from the most unexpected of places news of a whole new day of ecumenical encounter.

That the new view, the new daring, the new adventure should have come from the Catholic liturgists is natural enough. For in this sacrament-centered church it is through worship that it has its primary relations with its people. It is there the pressure has long been felt to catch up with the times, to speak the language of the day, to use symbols meaningful for today.

All the world knows, now, what has happened. The newspapers are full of it. The magazines have covered it. Books by the score have been written upon it. The mighty church of Rome has been making some changes. The bishops, gathered in Vatican Council, have been fairly up in arms to make long-needed changes. And most significant to Protestants are the changes in worship.

It has now been decreed that the preaching of the Word shall be part of every mass, and that mass itself will have many sections read in the language of the people. And in more and more churches the priest is facing his people from behind the altar, an altar which by symbol and use has become a table.

In Minnesota, in a suburb of Minneapolis, a local Catholic priest was not only invited, but accepted an invitation to attend the installation council of a neighboring Congregational minister. Not only did he come and mingle with the ministers and guests, but he was willing to be voted in as an honorary member of that Protestant ecclesiastical council, with both voice and vote—surely an historic landmark in Congregational ecumenicity, and perhaps a landmark from the Catholic side as well.

A confirmation class, visiting a neighboring Catholic church, were struck by the changes since just a year before. Not only was much of the service said in English, and not only did the priest preach, and say mass from behind the table with his face to the people—but a layman sat in the altar area and opened up "the Word" and read them the Scriptures. Changes there are, and very real ones there are.

In the city of Minneapolis in the fall of 1963, a group of Protestant ministers gathered for breakfast together. One of them had brought a friend as special guest and speaker, a Catholic priest: a Catholic priest who had been steeping himself in the history and meaning of the liturgy of his church. In this field he was an expert. He had also seen the implications of the new liberalism in Catholic liturgical revival and he was spreading the message. He was introduced as a Catholic priest who believed in "justification by faith." We were rocked on our heels, for this could have been Luther speaking. Later, the same priest came and preached at a midweek evening Lenten service in a Protestant church—itself a significant departure from Roman exclusivism—and proceeded there to confess his own church's self-righteousness and sins of commission and omission down through the ages. And more than that, he addressed us as his brothers, his "dear friends in Christ." And we felt we were, that night.

And it is a singular experience for an ardent free churchman to visit a great Abbey Church in Minnesota and to have it explained in a private chapel below that the altar is a table and designed to be so, moved symbolically at least, out from the wall and with a design suggesting legs. The priest is telling you what you for years have been telling your people—the same symbols, the same reason: that Christ is in the midst, that he sat at a table and therefore welcomes men to it, that they sit around it in symbol of supper and the fellowship of that meal. Curious that a Catholic priest who most of his life had been celebrating mass with his back to the people, before something he called an altar, should be explaining the importance of the table and of facing the people, to a Congregational minister whose whole heritage insisted it was a table, a table where the minister faced his people!

They are seeing here the meaning of worship as we see it. They are excited about the sweep and the movement and the place of the people in it, as we are. They are traveling our road, the one we travel now, the one we've traveled for three hundred years!

Why so? How can it be possible? Because, I believe, and its logic seems irrefutable—for reform of their church they are turning where the free churches too once turned, for the reform of their church: to the Bible, and the Book of Acts, and the New Testament church. They are not so much becoming Protestant in their views as they are becoming more New Testament in their views. Under the guidance of the Holy Spirit, they have opened up the Scripture and are being led to see what the free church fathers of the Puritan and Separatist movements of England saw three hundred years ago. They are seeing the picture of a first-century church that was the people's church, a church in which the Holy Spirit moved and had great power—a church that exalted "Holy Spirit" above "Holy church." And the lesson is not being lost. They see an independence of life, a vitality of congregations, a place held by laymen, and sacraments shared in freely.

This is no preserve of the free churches! This is no private bailiwick of the gathered church! But it happens to be a "way" they have loved and lived, a kind of worship to which they have tried to be faithful, a way of life they have tried to preserve.

They have preserved it, I think, unknowingly. And in the pressures of ecumenical days many of them have clung to it selfishly. Others have forgotten it, or eschewed it, and said that the mission of the "free" churches, the "congregational" churches, was to die to their old way in order to find new life in the ecumenical church. And so a great heritage was discarded.

But here now is the great church of Rome walking, in some very significant ways, the road we walked. And curiously, Rome is not alone. Creative leaders even from the Anglican church have sensed the need for a new symbolism, a new understanding of worship. They have begun to call for a new view of worship in their own church, where the priests would, as with the Romans, face the people for the service, and recognize Christ as in the midst.

Canon Southcott, formerly of Leeds, tells exciting tales in his *Parish Comes Alive* of a church being renewed by a new attempt to do in worship what is actually happening. Therefore, the Bible is held aloft and brought in in procession to a prominent place on the altar. Baptism is brought straight to the heart of the people's life by moving the font front and center, permanently, to remind the people of their role in baptism. And then, of course, he has had the most delightful experience of gathering meetings of the whole parish to decide after prayer and discussion what was to be done, rather than leaving it to the vestry. The exciting results he had no idea were the long-standing practice of the gathered churches in what they call the "church meeting."

Pioneers from the Left

So the revolution rolls on. It is reformation and renewal in an exciting new day. But the big surprise, which few have understood, particularly among the most advanced Protestant ecumenical leaders, is that the new direction Rome has taken liturgically is putting her on a more common New Testament basis and understanding with the free churches, the gathered churches, the churches of the Protestant left, than with the more obviously similar churches liturgically, at the Protestant right. It is the Spirit and what it can do in the church that more and more is leading Catholics into serious conversation with free churchmen.

For it is those free churchmen who have what most interests and intrigues the theologians of Rome today. It is they who have in their own life the concepts of ministry and worship which come from the same growing edge of the New Testament that Rome is walking today.

It will be a challenge to Rome, and it will be a challenge to the Protestant ecumenical churches. But it will be a challenge far more to the gathered churches themselves, who, in many respects, have considered themselves outcasts of the ecumenical movement. The challenge to them will be to see who they really are and what they really have; a challenge to move out—armed with this gift and knowledge—into the main stream of encounter.

If they do it faithfully, the free churches may share significantly in the recovery of meaning and power and the joy of the Spirit, in the life of worship of the whole church in the new day that is coming.

6

The Gathered Church and the Mission in the World

The excitement in the contemporary movement for renewal does not stop with worship. Liturgical renewal has been but an opening door for the renewal of the whole church: its assumptions, its purposes, its very life. And primary in all of this has been an attack upon the church's mission, a criticism of the church's failure to take the message of Christ literally into all the world—into every segment of society's life.

Nothing appears to be sacrosanct any more. No belief, no tradition, no practice is free from examination, closed to question or doubt, immune to criticism or attack. In the Catholic Church the revolution in theology has allowed questions to be raised on every subject from papal infallibility to clerical celibacy and birth control. And in Protestantism the debate has gone so far as to raise questions about the validity of the institution of the church itself.

The Mission in the World 101

The Contemporary Debate

For a whole generation the critique has been growing. It was probably Swiss theologian Karl Barth who threw the first bombshell back in 1927 with his book on *Romans*. He saw a God above the church whose Word must be "thrown at people's heads" without warning or preparation. This God made demands on men from outside themselves, and from outside their world, and from outside their little institutions, and they must respond to this "Word of God" with a "Yes" or a "No." No longer could they rest in the natural religion of an earlier generation where the easy assumptions of nineteenth-century liberalism viewed the world as getting better and better and all of life as a kind of scientific progression up to God. This attack upon the naïve social and theological assumptions of the early twentieth century was the opening volley in a war that is still being waged. The horror of economic disaster and the ravages of the demonic powers let loose from Hitler's Germany dispelled whatever easy illusions were left. The church in Germany proved weak in its days of crisis, and the suspicion began to spread, when the war was over, that there was weakness and irrelevance in the church around the world—and particularly in the church of the Western World.

In America, the postwar years brought affluence, and conformity, and fear of being different, a national lack of high purpose, and oddly enough—perhaps out of the great insecurity following war—a vast increase in church attendance and a kind of religious revival.

But the 1960's have brought at last a new day. Not only will they be America's most exciting and revolutionary political decade, but they are destined apparently to be her most radical religious decade as well. For the first time since the shock and shattering of the Second World War is America and the American religious mind able spiritually to think about the radical implications of the original Barthian insights.

It is in the late 1950's and early 1960's that a young student of Karl Barth, the martyred German theologian, Dietrich Bonhoeffer, has come into his own. His writings have deeply influenced the young theologians and church leaders of today. And his cry has been for a "religionless Christianity," a Christianity set free from its often archaic institutional forms to move out creatively into the secular society to influence men, not in the Sunday morning piety of the public worship hour, but out where they live, and move, and have their being in office and shop, in political party and corporation boardroom, at the novelist's typewriter and the artist's easel.

—Not that nothing has happened since Barth first wrote, or since Bonhoeffer was hanged at Flossenburg, or since the World War ended. The cry for a contemporary Christianity was heard long since, and remarkable new movements toward a contemporary witness have been emerging in the modern world. They have been movements to match the new age: the age of atomic fission and space travel, the age of power on a physical, scientific, institutional, and social scale never before seen among men. They particularly have been movements to reach the mass man, the man of the world's cities, where more and more of the world's population live.

In Germany itself came the Kirchentag, the gigantic German Christian layman's movement. In Scotland came George MacLeod and the Iona Community. In America came George Webber, Don Benedict, Archie Hargreaves, and the East Harlem Protestant Parish: each one a mission mounted to challenge the church to meet the needs of the new mass man. In East Harlem it was a radical new approach to the innercity man through the medium of store-front churches— churches operating visibly at the street level where minister and people could be in direct contact with the masses of people they were there to reach and to serve. It was a mission to try to reclaim for the Protestant witness a vast segment of society previously abandoned. It was an attempt through dramatic new means to mount a mission to the man of the central city.

On the isle of Iona it was again an attempt to stage a mission of the church in a new way in a new day to the workingman of the industrial cities of Scotland where the traditional churches seemed unable to reach. The Iona method was to gather young clergy into a disciplined brotherhood or community of work and worship out on the holy isle of Iona during the summers, in order to prepare themselves, both by their physical labor and their sense of common discipline through prayer, to go into the industrial areas; it was also a new look at worship and at the power of intercessory prayer to bring reconciliation and transformation.

In Germany the Kirchentag brought lay Christians together in great mass meetings to learn and to witness to their faith. It also gathered Christians together in lay academies for a whole rethinking of their faith and witness in a radically changed world.

These were among the earliest creative postwar attempts to find new means of mission for the Christian Church. Others too have found their way into being. Gordon Cosby and his Church of the Saviour in Washington, D.C., with its two-year preparation for church membership, and its mission of the people through its coffeehouse, "The Potter's Wheel," would have to be counted among the more radical attempts in America to follow Iona and East Harlem into mission. Reuel Howe and his training center in Michigan has been another creative attempt to rethink the place of the layman in the church and to develop a theology of mission. Its influence upon such thinkers as sociologist Gibson Winter, author of *The Suburban Captivity of the Churches*, has been profound. William Hollister and his Presbyterian church in Burlington, Vermont, which have consistently refused to build a building but meet for worship instead in the city jail, run as well a coffeehouse called "The Loft" in downtown Burlington and "The Jazz Barn" on the campus of the University of Vermont as ways of reaching the secular culture, stand too among the more radical ventures of the postwar American church.

And yet in the 1960's the findings of these experimental ministries had become almost common knowledge through the American church. Their witness has so permeated the church's awareness and so influenced a new generation of younger thinkers and theologians that, for the first time, a radical protest is being widely made and widely heard for not only a few isolated, creative, experimental ministries but for a radical restructuring of the entire church—a restructuring of its very form and life.

These avant-garde thinkers see the old structures standing in the way of the new ideas and their creative possibilities. They see ecclesiastical superiors in denominations thwarting the experimental and creative in their baliwicks because "they interfere with the program of the church." They see the leaders of local congregations also resisting and obstructing, if possible, attempts to restructure church life, claiming they do so on the grounds that their own position and very jobs are being threatened.

For these men it is a call to mission. It is a call to a whole new form for the church's life. As the magazine *Renewal* states: "The stage for debate is set: in an era of change, what kind of church? In a world of personal and social disease, what character of ministry? In a period when diffused energies only perpetuate and deepen confusion and decay, what are the vital thrusts, the positive programs, the crucial understandings?" [1]

The burden of the criticism of many of the young spokesmen is that in order to achieve renewal, in order to set the laity free for their total mission, in order to meet the new structures of our complex society, the local congregation as a means of

[1] *Renewal*, December, 1963, p. 4.

mission, indeed of life for the church, must be done away—
that it is no longer relevant to the society it is trying to serve.
Again, the magazine *Renewal* draws clear the lines when it
reports:

> The emerging debate centers on the nature of the Church,
> and of the individual congregation within the Church. The
> reason for debate is that the working out of a positive Church
> program in this decade will threaten the existence of established
> structures. . . .[2]

For better or worse, then, the church in America is involved
in a debate about its own future—about whether it can be
geared for mission or not, about whether it can meet the new
demands of a new day or not, and about whether it can finally
survive in its present form or not.

And the form of the church's life apparently most open to
question, most marked for extinction, most irrelevant for the
present concept of mission, is the congregation, the local
residential church. The question of mission in the 1960's in
the eyes of the young theologians and experimenters has become a question of doing away with the outmoded structure
of the residential parish church and finding new and presumably more appropriate means of mission, a question of trading
the residential church for the chaplaincy in industry, the
specialized ministry in hospital and factory, in market place
and theater, in night spot and shopping center.

Highly influential in the thinking of those who would reform the local church is the theory of sociologist Gibson
Winters, who suggests in his *Suburban Captivity' of the
Churches* that cities should be divided into pie-shaped sectors
striking along radial lines from the suburbs into the heart
of the city with mission mounted from the more affluent
Christians of the suburbs into the areas of greatest need in the
city's core. There would be no parish churches but rather

[2] *Renewal*, December, 1963, p. 6.

gatherings of Christians for study and fellowship in small home groups, or office, or professional, or other groups. Small office buildings might be maintained within the sector with some facility for teaching of children and the giving of direction to the people's mission. Public worship for all the Christians in the sector would be provided by one or two large cathedral churches where all might gather, rich and poor, intellectual and simple to hear the "finest" of preaching instead of the mediocre message which the critics are convinced is all the world hears in most parish churches.

The plan may have some merit. It would direct the passion and concern and faith of suburban Christians toward the central city where they work, where their cultural life is nourished, where their income is derived, but where their personal concern for people has not been.

It is a plan that has been seriously considered. But is it the answer? Will it renew the life of the church in our time? Will it go into all the world and preach the gospel? Will it comfort the broken-hearted, and set free the captives, and proclaim the acceptable year of the Lord? Will it do these things in the world which the new generation wants, and which the church historically has taken as its mission?

I believe it cannot. And the reason it cannot is because of a fatal fallacy in its thinking. Its plan is beautiful, its manipulations would be ingenious. But it forgets that the church of Christ is made up of people: people called into fellowship with him by Christ—people who need a pastor; people who come into the life of the church because of their need, as well as their desire to serve; people who long to be part of a company, who long to have comrades, who yearn to be friends of "the Way" with companions of the covenant. It is a plan that forgets the need of Christian people to be a family as well as a force, a band of brothers as well as an army, a company of comrades as well as a mighty mission.

The Fatal Fallacy

The fallacy is one of faith. It is one of forgetting the need of millions to be fed the bread of life, to be cared about, and to be cared for. It is the fallacy of forgetting that an army must still be fed, that it must still be nourished, that it must still be made strong for the fight.

How do you feed an army of the Lord? How do you heal, and comfort, and strengthen, and inspire disciples? How do you fashion them into fighting men? How do you equip and field soldiers for the Saviour?

You do not really do it by pushing anybody and everybody out into the field at once. You teach, you train, you send out scouting parties, you send out patrols, you teach and train some more, you equip a light cavalry unit and send them out. More and more are prepared, and more and more are sent out.

The Fallacy of the Faith

The first part of the fallacy, then, is to think that the whole church is ready to be sent out into the world, out into the secular society, out into the public sector of government, and business, the professions, and the arts, without any means for the nurturing of their own faith.

Cut away the congregations from the life of this pie-shaped wedge of the church's mission into the central city, and where and how would the people's faith be born or be nurtured and nourished, built up and strengthened? Would all Christians suddenly sign up for courses at the Cathedral Church? Would they all even go to services in the Cathedral? Would each one be even more diligent in his duty to pore over the Scriptures daily, to read the classics of devotion, and to fall to his knees in prayer?

He should. Indeed, he should! But if we know our humankind at all, we know very well that they would not. The plain fact is that the church was given, among many things, for the nurturing and encouraging and challenging of the lives of men. And without this spur to their faith there is grave doubt that there would ever have been a church or a faith to last all these two thousand years. The Lord has given us the church—and particularly here, the local, gathered church, where men live, and move, and worship, and work—to keep the faith of Christians alive, to encourage them in their faith and discipline, to inspire and challenge them and keep them free, and alive, and growing.

And this is the element that has been found wanting in contemporary, ecumenically minded Christianity, by the evangelicals, the "conservatives." They have looked at the rising tide of criticism of church and the growing movement for reform and renewal of the church, and they say, "But where is the faith? Where is the very motivating power with which you hope to do all these things? What are you going to say to the world when you get there? What will your message be when you sit in the boardroom of the corporation, or when you face the artist at his easel, or the housewife in her kitchen? Will you have a message for them? Will you have a real Christ who died and lives again for man? Will you offer them a real salvation, an honest change in sinful life—a change great enough in their life so that they, in Christ's name, can change the world's life?"

The great fear of the conservative evangelicals, as they look out upon the church's increasing emphasis both on experimental ministries and on ministries of radical mission and social action, is that "the faith" will be lost. They listen to these young men, talking about a "secular gospel" and a "religionless Christianity," and they listen to their testimony to the faith that is in them and they suspect that what they are hearing is a strange new double-talk. They suspect that when these men talk of the "event" of Christ, what they really mean is that Christ does not have to have lived at all, and that

The Mission in the World

the Christ these men speak of is a dead Christ—just an idea—and not a real and living Person alive today.

The evangelicals look at the mainline churches of Protestantism today and sense in their drive for renewal, secular relevance, and a new knowledge and appreciation of the world, a rising apostacy—a throwing over of the essential faith altogether. In the words of Dr. Carl Henry, editor of *Christianity Today*: "They're all sick." [3]

And yet the evangelicals are not beyond the pale of the world-wide movement for church reform, either. They are, generally, a far different crowd from the "fundamentalists" of the 1930's. They too are sensing the sweeping tide of a new spirit in American church life. Their evangelism has grown up, it has taken into account the modern world, and it has moved effectively and powerfully to meet the modern man. Their approaches to the mass man, to high school students, to university campuses, to laymen in the churches, and to the whole need for Bible study have become themselves some of the new techniques and strategy that mark the present decade of Christian reform and renewal. Emancipation from the legalisms of the past is evident with Dr. William Bright, director of the powerful *Campus Crusade for Christ*, when he says, "Legalism somehow is death." [4]

Nor do they, in their most responsible leadership, stand any more for an oversimplified "faith versus works" sort of emphasis. They do not want to sacrifice the faith, the burning heart of their Christian message. But at the same time they are not antiaction either. They are not all segregationists. They are not all against the church having political and social concerns, as well as theological ones. A surprising number of them are even leaving the hard-core fundamental churches of their birth and upbringing precisely because these churches, as they say,

---

[3] Quoted in *Look*, July 27, 1965, p. 18, an article on "The Battle of the Bible."
[4] *Op. cit.*, p. 20.

have become "gospel-hardened"; the Spirit no longer moves freely, and the church no longer seems to care about the world. They are moving instead into churches, in some cases, which may have a tradition of liberal spirit, and liberal social and political concern, but which preach and believe a faith in a present and powerful living Christ. Something new and unusual is happening to old-line fundamentalism in America. Dr. Billy Graham himself is claiming that "the biggest story of our time" is the emergence of a "completely new man," the "believing activist," whose purpose is to "change the world." [5]

Evangelicals and liberals are finding a common interest in the exciting new "troubling of the waters" of our time, where the renewal in liturgy, and the mounting movement for racial justice, and the attempt to find new forms for the church's mission are all being melted into one new phenomenon of the 1960's seen as a "new Reformation," a new age of the Spirit's power.

But the conservative evangelicals are cautious because of their concern for the faith, because of their concern to see men's hearts and lives changed as well as their opportunities for education, and their right to vote, and their situation of poverty and prejudice changed. Their influence could be powerful and real in making this "new Reformation" complete if their one great concern—a completely justified and essential one—were taken seriously and acted upon: their concern for a great faith for an exciting, fast-changing world.

The first fallacy of the young leaders who call for an end to the residential congregation as a means of mission and a restructuring of the entire church is their failure to be very much concerned, either about the faith itself, or the nurturing and developing in the lives of people a faith that could change the world.

[5] Quoted in *op. cit.*, p. 18.

The Fallacy of the Church

The second fallacy in such thinking is the failure to recognize the historic effectiveness of the residential congregation not only as an instrument for teaching of the faith and for nurturing it through worship and fellowship in the life of the congregation, but also as an instrument for mission and renewal itself.

As such a weapon in the battle for a new life in the church the local congregation has already been discounted as of little value by many of the most radical and most adventurous innovators.

Surely any pastor who has loved and cared for a congregation of God's people, and any layman who has been one of those people, knows full well the sins of the church: knows very well that the residential congregation, like the residential family, is not perfect and is full of sin. But he also knows that the church at that level, just like the family at that level, offers something to the whole church and the whole world that no other institution can.

Here is where people are changed, slowly and painfully. Here is where new ideas do grow, slowly and painfully. Here is where the Spirit moves, when God's people seek him, with sometimes sudden and all-consuming power. Here is where not only renewal but revival can break out, and can radically alter a people's whole direction of service and ministry. Here is where the most profound and crucial needs of life can be met because here is where God's people are. Here is where Christ's missionaries in the world do, in fact, meet and worship together, do in fact share the sacraments of the Lord's Supper and Christian Baptism together, do in fact eat at table, share ideas, read the Bible and pray together, and finally, with comforting hand and encouraging word do mount the Church's mission and move out into the world to perform it, for Jesus' sake.

If Christians were to meet *only* in professional or business groups, where would the sacraments be celebrated, where would the Word be preached, where would Christian men enter into covenant obligation with each other? Where else, but in the local church? Where else, frankly, but in the gathered church?

The Gathered Church as a Vehicle for Mission

Many there are who have not despaired of the local church—even as a base for mission. David Colwell, pastor of Washington's First Congregational Church, says, "Let's fight the battles within the congregation." "My feeling," says Colwell, "is that if there is any real preaching being done today, it's being done by parish parsons who have guts enough to say the truth." Note: "parish" parsons. Parsons who are not safe and protected behind the broad desk of a denominational executive office or behind the podium in the lecture room of a theological seminary professor: but exposed and vulnerable out on the firing line of the church, out where they can be shot down both by the people of the church and the people of the world.

Perhaps the local church of God's people, gathered together by Christ to know him and to know each other, to live together and love together and be the church together, is both the most dangerous and most exciting place a Christian minister or a Christian layman could be. Maybe this is where great things will happen if they will happen anywhere. Maybe this is where the greatest risks will be taken if they are going to be taken anywhere. Maybe this is where the most successful mission can be launched if it is to be launched anywhere.

Local congregations are more able to move, to act, significantly and powerfully, and in obedience to the Lord of the church, than are the slow-moving cumbersome defenders of the *status quo*, the denominations. When the call of Christ is

The Mission in the World

clearest and the church is most obviously called to arms, it is the local church and the individual Christian—lay and clerical—who can and do move most rapidly and most effectively. The witness may be small and unorganized, but it is powerful and transforming.

The churches of the gathered tradition take most seriously the doctrine of "the priesthood of all believers," and preserve a tradition of individualism in faith based on the right and duty of every member to interpret the Scriptures—and their ethical demands—according to the guidance that the Holy Spirit gives him. The impact of the churches being open in their individualism to the free power of the risen Christ in our time far outweighs the misguided use of that freedom.

The local church, the residential congregation, can move and can be a creative vehicle for mission—particularly when that local church is of the gathered tradition, the tradition that casts its own independency utterly upon the mercy and the might of Christ. The power of the gathered church is in the fact that it bears full responsibility. No official of an ecclesiastical hierarchy, nor even a book of laws, canon or otherwise, can either direct a local church in its action or rescue it if it has taken unwise action. The responsibility for its life under God is its own.

Therefore, it must seek the mind and will of Christ perhaps more frequently and more diligently than more authoritarian churches. And it must so organize its life that the free-moving Spirit of Christ will find it most sensitive and most open to his will. The Church Meeting of all the members, therefore, becomes that assembly in which all the people's concerns are most carefully and conscientiously brought to light for free discussion and, if possible, unanimous decision.

Such a church, such a form of the church's life—at that point where men "live and move and have their being"—has open to it peculiar opportunities both for bringing about the renewal of the church and for being a viable means for the church's daily, week-by-week commission in the world. The temptation of the denominational and hierarchical church is to wait until the denomination moves, and to act in those areas which the denomination suggests. But the gathered church, bearing full responsibility for its own life and witness, is free to respond to the needs as they arise, either on the local or the national level. Is there a human need not being met in the neighborhood? The gathered church is free to meet it. Is there a cooperative effort, an association of churches needed in order to do a job or fulfill a mission? The gathered church can move immediately without costly delay in securing permission of the denomination or board. Like a light cavalry, flexible and free-wheeling, the gathered church is prepared as an army to move when the Spirit calls and where the Spirit calls.

In 1865, in the first national gathering of free churchmen of the Congregational order at Boston and Plymouth, the way of the gathered church, congregational in form, was offered to America as a way for a newly emancipated nation to walk in: a way for freedom, following the free movement of God's free Spirit. They said,

> Wherever devout and believing souls, weary of hierarchical and synodical governments over Christ's free people, are ready to unite in a church which shall be only Christ's, and in which they may joyfully learn and testify that where the Spirit of the Lord is there is liberty. . . .[6]

There they would be to welcome them. The only true church, in their view, was made up of:

> assemblies of believers and worshippers, holding what is essential to Christian faith.

And such a church

> . . . is rightfully governed by no pretended vicar of Christ, nor

[6] From Preface to the *Platform of 1865*.

by any assembly having jurisdiction over particular churches, but only by Christ Himself through His Word and Spirit.

The only visible church, according to them, was local or parochial:

> a congregation of believers dwelling together in one city, town, or convenient neighborhood.[7]

It was this church where, they believed, the whole work of the church could be done, the whole mission carried out, the most effective renewal carried on.

And the ecumenical principle of such a concept of the Christian church is that obviously, every organization, every structure of the church's life has, at some point, a structure like this: a local congregation, a gathering of Christian people who worship together and work together and who strive to fulfill the church's mission together.

The gift of the gathered church is to offer this as the unique and most powerful and most Christian unit and form of church life to the whole church. Its gift is to say, "Look, see what you have! You all have it—Roman Catholics, Lutherans, Episcopalians, Presbyterians, and Methodists alike. These gathered churches of God's people are common to us all. And under the guidance of the Holy Spirit they can be your most flexible, fastest-moving vehicle of mission, because they are there. They are there where things are happening, where people are, where the needs are, and where the mission must be mounted if it is to be mounted at all. Try it and see! We do not give it to you—you already have it. It is just that we have kept it alive at the heart and center of our life while you have kept it at the periphery of yours. But give the gathered church a chance. It is the one vital unit of life we all share. And if you will trust it to the Spirit, it can become the church's outpost of mission in every town. Try it and see!"

[7] From Chapter II, pp. 4, 5, of Preliminary Principles, *Platform of 1865*.

The problem, of course, is that many denominational leaders have tended to give up on the local church as a front-line mission. They have ambivalent feelings about it. They use it. They manipulate it. It is the object of all their promotion and programs. But rarely have they trusted it. Rarely have they said to the local church: "Obviously you know the needs of your community better than we. You know what is most needing to be done. You go ahead with the mission as you see it. We trust you. We know the Holy Spirit will guide you. We leave you to him. God bless you! If we can help you with our resources, let us know!"

Quite a different thing from the concept of congregations as merely "outlets" for a vast organization, or as the lowest level in a chain of command. And yet, when they are put on their honor to do it, some of the most creative thinking in the whole church's life comes out of local congregations. That is, when officials and ministers alike make it plain that they want such creative contribution and participation.

I do not mean to suggest it is all with the local congregation. Its temptations to parochialism are huge. Many local churches are not creative. And some very exciting experiments in church renewal have succeeded only because once conceived, they were financially supported by denominational funds. The East Harlem Protestant Parish is an example.

And yet the creative thrust was not denominational. It came from the vision of a few. The new approaches of the E.H.P.P. were fashioned, and honed, and tested *in a parish*, in *gathered congregations* by dedicated, daring, and undefeated young men. William Hollister's Presbyterian Church in Burlington, Vermont was planted by denominational planners, but the genius, the imagination with its Jazz Barn, its Loft, and its regular worship in the city jail was that congregation's creativity and faith. The Church of the Saviour in Washington, D.C., was one man's dream. The remarkable Tamworth Association, where a Baptist, Congregational, and Episcopal

Church in three New Hampshire towns have shared one minister and a common parish life for over ten years is also the dream of one man and the determination and broad spirit of another.

Where Christian people—of whatever denomination—have been free in local, gathered churches, to follow the leading of the Holy Spirit into adventures of faith, they have tended to move faster and more successfully than have programs fostered at "higher" levels of church structure. The ecumenical movement in America today, with even the Roman Catholic Church finding previously unheard-of freedom, is producing tremendously exciting experiments and encounters in Christian fellowship and action at the local level. Not because denominational or chancery offices are urging it but because the Holy Spirit of God is touching people where they live, in gathered congregations, and making it happen.

The crucial question is one of trust and of willingness to depend utterly upon the power of the Holy Spirit to work his will through his church.

The experience of more and more pastors is that when, in faith, they take their hands off the machinery of the church, and stop manipulating everything, that is when Jesus Christ has a chance to work in the church and when, by his power, miracles of new life begin to happen.

I know one pastor who can testify that in his suburban church more creative mission took place in one year when he let God move than he had accomplished in years of his own pushing and shoving!

During that year God's Spirit had a chance to work in the lives of people, bringing about their conversion and transformation in such a way that the whole congregation is beginning to feel the effect, and is seeing and meeting the needs of the community with a new and vital view of mission.

Jesus Christ can do these things when the church gives him a chance. The secret of life in the gathered church is that in depending completely upon the power and authority and guidance of Christ's spirit, the doors to that opportunity are opened up.

Where is the proof, you say? The proof is in the long history of the free churches in America, not proudly but gratefully told. Out of the life of these churches came the American Board of Commissioners for Foreign Missions, the first foreign mission board in this country. From these churches came also America's first Bible Society. In civil rights a hundred years ago these churches saw the need to throw bridges of understanding across the chasms of havoc and horror created by the Civil War.

Nor has the mission faded as a concern of the free churches in our time. In this very decade of the 1960's the churches of the gathered tradition still lead the way as missionary churches. Ecumenical figures no less distinguished than Dr. Henry Pitney Van Dusen, President Emeritus of Union Theological Seminary, documented not long ago in the *Christian Century* the fact that the one group of Christians in all South America making headway in spreading the Christian faith and the Christian church was not the Roman Catholic Church with its cadres of dedicated priests and nuns, and not the mainline ecumenical Protestant denominations with their rather formal missionary programs, but was instead the passionately committed, deeply believing, and utterly self-sacrificing evangelical conservative churches! The missionaries of these churches are going where few others dare to go. They are making sacrifices few others are willing to make, and they are winning converts to Christ as no other group of churches is doing. The story of the mission to the Auca Indians of Ecuador is just one example of their Christian heroism.

In all parts of the world the missionaries of the free denominations, those whose life centers in gathered churches, are making the same impact and moving with the same power.

Historically in America the whole movement of evangelism

The Mission in the World

has been taken most seriously and been used most successfully by Christians of the gathered churches. Dr. Billy Graham himself, surely the greatest evangelist of this century and perhaps of many centuries, is of the Baptist tradition.

Some skeptically discount these people as "just a bunch of fundamentalists." But, for better or worse, it is they who have carried the banner for mission and who have been most deeply committed to its cause. One of their churches, a great Congregational church in Boston, supports over one hundred missionaries in the field. You don't do this unless you take very seriously Jesus' charge laid upon us all: "Go ye into all the world, and preach the gospel."

Interestingly enough, it is the Christians of the free tradition who have been most concerned with Christ as a Person and least concerned with the church as an organization. Where the dead hand of bureaucracy and organizational machinery so often kills the real spirit and power of a movement, these Christians are those who have been most willing to support Christian work that is beyond denominational attachment, and made up of Christians who care, whatever their tradition. So have grown the highly effective organizations of evangelism and mission as the Billy Graham organization, Young Life, Campus Crusade for Christ, the Navigators, Christian Businessmen, and International Christian Leadership. And each of these has been ecumenical from the beginning, welcoming all who want to serve in faith, no matter what their denomination or tradition.

Many may still believe the only "relevant" mission, and social action, and renewal will come from the denominational planners and the denominationally supported experimental ministries. But if the church can believe in its Lord and trust his power to move, we may yet see an ecumenical and missionary day when local congregations of God's people all across the land will take fire and become the newest and yet oldest means of mission in the Christian church.

The Gathered Church and the Missionary Concern

The purpose of mission has always been the changing of the world. The ecumenical movement of the churches, the new stirring in the land, is a yearning to change the world—to transform an unjust society and enliven an irrelevant church.

Experience has made many despair of the congregation as a means of mission. But the gathered churches stand as testimony that out of even very narrow and parochial local churches can come some of the most creative power for the renewal of the church and for carrying out its mission in the world.

Its principle is the power of the Holy Spirit to work directly, according to his promise, among the two or three believers gathered together, and to bring from them the faithful and renewing energies that the church so needs today. It does not exalt independence. It exalts openness to the leading of the Spirit. It exalts the freedom to move and the flexibility which a local church, operating at the grass roots of life and under the power of the Spirit, can achieve.

It asks the whole church to see with new eyes what it has seen a long time, and to understand more profoundly the dynamics of spiritual power at work. Many who themselves cry for more organization and authority do not realize that frequently the source of their own opportunity was a freedom in church life which the gathered church gave.

The local churches of the land with their strong voice to laymen and their many blind spots and subtle temptations are nevertheless not the hopelessly conservative and impossible institutions they have been thought to be. They have deep roots in Christian concern. They have great generosity, and a deep reservoir of desire to give and to serve.

That profound faith and compassionate spirit of the tradition of the gathered churches of America were expressed

The Mission in the World

prophetically in that "Burial Hill Declaration of Faith" [8] a hundred years ago. The great war between the states was over with its ruin left for all to see. President Lincoln had been assassinated. It was against this background that these men of free churches expressed their missionary concern:

> In the times that are before us as a nation, times at once of duty and of danger, we rest all our hope in the Gospel of the Son of God. It was the grand peculiarity of our Puritan Fathers, that they held this Gospel, not merely as the ground of their personal salvation, but as declaring the worth of man by the incarnation and sacrifice of the Son of God; and therefore applied its principles to elevate society, to regulate education, to civilize humanity, to purify law, to reform the church and the state, and to assert and defend liberty; in short, to mould and redeem, by its all-transforming energy, everything that belongs to man in his individual and social relations.
>
> It was the faith of our fathers that gave us this free land in which we dwell. It is by this faith only that we can transmit to our children a free and happy, because a Christian, commonwealth.

Renewal and mission have long then been the concern of the gathered church. Perhaps in this day of renewal and exciting new mission these churches have a way to point in which the whole church can follow.

[8] Adopted by the First National Council of the Congregational Churches in America, meeting on the old Plymouth Colony's Burial Hill in Plymouth, Massachusetts on June 22, 1865.

7

The Gathered Church and the Spirit's Power

As the people of God look toward the new structures and the new relationships which could someday draw all those who name the name of Christ together into one living fellowship, it is inevitable that we ask "Who are we? What kind of institution are we meant to be in the world, really? What are we supposed to do? What will our forms be for? What should the secret of our power be?" The ecumenical task is to get down to fundamentals, to the basics of the church, to see, if we can, who we were called to be, and what, if any, is our uniqueness.

Are we to be, for instance, a smooth-running, well-oiled machine? Are we to be primarily an organization, an institution dedicated to the service of God? Or are we to be, ultimately, something far less tangible, something much less definable, but something—in human and divine terms—far more real?

Are we a corporate structure, or are we a band of brothers? Are we men of the mind, or are we held together by the heart?

The Spirit's Power

Are we primarily an organization, or are we a great movement infused by a Spirit?

If we are to be honest with ourselves, and if we are to read the New Testament carefully, there is no other conclusion we can draw but that when all is said and done, when every good word has been put in for organizational efficiency, and technical competence, and expert know-how, the church of Jesus Christ is now and has always been primarily a movement of the Spirit, a company composed of comrades, a home for the heart and its hope. You could offer many qualifying statements, you could try very hard for a sense of balance, but in the end you would have to say: "The essential of the church is something in the Spirit, something God gives, something beyond man either to make or to give. The essential of the church is supernatural or spiritual. Without that it is nothing. Without that it is dead."

The Sense of the Spirit

I had the privilege once of breakfasting with a Russian Christian from the Soviet Union. Three hundred ministers of Minneapolis were gathered there to meet a delegation of Russians spending a month in the United States visiting our churches and people.

In Denver they were booed. In Minneapolis they were picketed. Some Americans could not see how they could live under the Soviet brand of atheistic communism and still call themselves Christians.

But during this minister's breakfast we sang several hymns together, and I discovered that my companion, a professor at the Leningrad Theological Institution who could speak a little English, was singing too. He had never seen our hymns before, but his hands were keeping time, and he was singing all the words he could. And then I noticed, on the second hymn, that halfway through—with deep feeling—he made the sign of the cross and seemed to be much moved. When the hymn was over he couldn't wait to point, with tears in his eyes, to the words he had seen, "Faith of our fathers living still, In spite of dungeon, fire, and sword . . . We will be true to Thee 'till death!" And he said to me: "This is very true—this is very true in my country!"

I have thought many times of my friend in Russia. As an official, free institution the church in that land is virtually dead. It has been harassed, and persecuted, and apparently snuffed out. But my friend "keeps the faith." What the government has done to him and to many other Christians, I do not know. I only know that long after the institution of the church has died in a land, that which is most truly the church lives on in "a man's heart." "Nothing shall be able to separate us," Paul said, "from the love of God, which is in Christ Jesus our Lord."

A missionary executive in America who was sent to look over the damage done in Angola where he once had served, after the uprising and the repression of the Christian church by the Portuguese government, reported a very curious thing. "Where the church's ministry had been primarily to plant institutions, to build schools and hospitals and denominational structure, the church was destroyed. They had only to kill the superintendent or the principal and the whole institution collapsed. But," he said, "where the church had planted Christians—where people had been taught to know Christ, there the church was still alive, still witnessing." He confessed it had been a salutary lesson to him. The essence of the church is in the faith, in the Spirit.

It is that sense of the spirit that is central to what the church of Jesus Christ is all about. Its point of persuasion in the lives of men, that which finally is touched, moved, "reached," converted, is always their spirit—that indefinable something within them that, out of the depths, responds. The church's own source of power had always been the Spirit. "I

The Spirit's Power

will pour out my spirit upon all flesh," God promised to Joel, and on the day of Pentecost that Spirit was poured out upon the new Christian church. Indeed, Jesus had commanded his friends to wait at Jerusalem until the Spirit was given. Obviously, the church would be able to do nothing without it. The Spirit was its source of power. And the vehicle for the carrying of that Spirit was the heart—the quality of life and love—of committed men.

The Christian church has never been anything without the Spirit! And the church has always known, and the world has always known, that whenever it lacked this quality it lacked everything. People very often cannot tell you why a particular local church does not appeal to them, and why they are leaving, but when pressed to their ultimate reasons, I am very sure their real answer is: "it does not have the Spirit—something is missing." The churches that are dull and irrelevant are the churches that do not have the Spirit; the churches that are doing important things in their mission and that grip people in their worship are churches that have it.

We are talking about the presence of Christ in the life of a church that claims to be Christian, and in the life of men who claim to be Christian.

Oddly enough, it is the secular world that often recognizes and honors the Spirit sooner than does the church. It was that world that saw it and recognized it in Jesus of Nazareth twenty centuries ago, when it said: "He taught them as one having authority and not as the scribes." He was different. The man of the Spirit is always different.

Jesus testified to this central quality of the Spirit which was to be the essence of his entire ministry when, on that day in Nazareth he chose, when called upon to read in the synagogue, the mighty words of Isaiah: "The Spirit of the Lord God is upon me, because he hath anointed me to preach the gospel...," and then sat down saying, "This day is this scripture fulfilled in your ears." And every eye was fastened upon him because they knew that something had happened there that day. They knew that a special power had come among them. A strange power—in this young man whom they had known as a boy.

Those in history who have been most true to him have also had something of this special power: something of his Spirit, the Holy Spirit which he gave to the world. All men recognize it. They recognize it in the quality of a man's love—a love which he has, as his Lord has, for common people. He has what the church today and the world today are hungry to have, in the church and in its ministry.

The sense of the Spirit is essential for the great church that is coming.

The Power of the Spirit

But even more than a "spiritual quality" and an awareness of the presence of the Spirit, the church needs desperately in the years just ahead the power of the Spirit. For the fact is that not all the manipulations, and arrangings, and "conversations," and mergers that men try can ever, by themselves, bring about the church where all Christians are truly one in the fellowship of the table, the family, the brotherhood, with no marks of distinction and with no walls of exclusion. If Christians in our day or any other day are ever united in essentials into one common band of brothers, no longer "separated," it will be the Holy Spirit that will make it so. It will be the power of the Holy Spirit unbending a lot of stiff Christians, opening a lot of blind eyes, and changing a lot of hard hearts, and making love and understanding so real that unity at the deepest levels will just "happen," will take place in such a way that no man will be able to do anything to stop it.

What is crucial to the ecumenical movement now is for all Christians of every tradition to recognize this. It is crucial for every Christian, and for every denomination, and for everyone who cares anything at all about the church and its renewal, to recognize that unity comes, "Not by might, nor by power, but *by my spirit.*" Christian unity cannot be manufactured, it cannot be forced. It can come only in God's way and by his power.

If Christians really believe this, or if they can come to believe it, then they will begin, in all their discussions and plans, to put more and more emphasis upon the Holy Spirit. They will think about how he works. They will remember that it moves "where it listeth," that no man can tell "whence it cometh or whither it goeth." They will expect him to do the unexpected. They will begin to look more carefully at the simple things of church life—at simpler people, simpler traditions, simpler forms and practices. They will begin to be a lot less prejudiced about what is "relevant" and what is not. They will begin to "become as little children"—a very difficult thing for great theologians, and for ecumenical statesmen, and for parish ministers, and for us all. Our whole basis of evaluating will be different.

As the church becomes more serious about the Holy Spirit, it will begin to see many important things whole again, and no longer fractured; it will begin to see many things in their essentials again, and no longer in their nonessentials; it will begin to see what is really important—what is important to Christ, and it will see far more clearly than before the few things that are really basic, that are really necessary and ultimate for unity in Christ. It will see that men with great differences of conviction and practice in nonessentials can be united in a simple desire to be true to Christ. Above all, the church will see that the Holy Spirit and its power can be depended upon: that given patience, and trust, and great faith, and a willingness to love, on the part of God's people, the Holy Spirit can be trusted to lead the church in each of its congregations and in each of its members into all truth, and into faithful witness, and into a powerful and redeeming and renewing ministry.

The church will be able to see, I think, that everything of eternal value that ever really does happen or ever has happened in the church's life happens by the power of this Spirit. When lives are changed the Spirit changes them. When prayer is answered the Spirit has brought that answer. When the church is faithful to its mission, it is because the Spirit has been in its midst.

The true church is where the Holy Spirit dwells among men. And when men come to the church looking for something that has reality about it, and power about it, and truth and love about it, they are, consciously or unconsciously, looking for the fruits of the Spirit.

The risen, living Christ is at work in the world. And he is not dependent upon anything but open and expectant hearts in order to do his work. That is why Jesus said: "Where two or three are gathered together in my name, there am I in the midst of them." The Spirit is not dependent upon popes or priests, upon hierarchies or apostolic successions, upon proper ordination or any other prerogative in order to do his work. He needs only the open heart of the believing man, and the expectant spirit of the gathered congregation.

Most important for the church today to understand is that the power of the Holy Spirit is the only single power and single authority that is recognized across every creed of Christendom. Men may be bound by a million rules or organized into narrow, unbending, rigid theologies, but one thing they are always able to recognize, one thing they are never quite able to deny, is the power of God's Spirit in another man's life. Whether he be pope or preacher, evangelist or monk, there is something, sometimes, that so marks a man's life that all who know him say: "He is a man of the Spirit."

Other claims to authority are not universally recognized: the right of bishops, the sacredness of dogma, the infallibility

The Spirit's Power

of the pope or the reliability of denominational pronouncements. But the power of the Spirit—that we cannot deny.

But it has also been recognized that the power of the Spirit is not always convenient in its demands upon men. It is sometimes exceedingly awkward in what it asks of them. It cannot be controlled by them. Consequently, very few forms of church life have been willing to subject themselves completely to the free movement of the Holy Spirit. Very few church traditions have dared to expose their collective life to its strange incursions from outside. They have felt it important that the free reign of the Spirit be balanced by some form of human mediation: by the wise counsel of an elected bishop, or by the collective wisdom of a council of men, a "session," or a presbytery, or a synod, or a college of cardinals. This, they felt, would protect the church from an independent congregation's temptations to anarchy, or to misreading of the Spirit's intentions, or other blind spots it could so easily have.

But the gathered churches have accepted this risk. Foolishly or not they have taken the chance. They have believed that the only way they could really do what Christ alone wanted them to do was by casting themselves utterly upon him, by devising a form of church life that would be completely open and sensitive to his will and direction.

They were supported in this conviction by the realization that the New Testament church, as far as they could discover from a faithful reading of the Scriptures, was such a church: a whole movement of local churches made up of gathered groups of believing Christians in different cities and towns: each church having a life of its own, and an independent status of its own, and yet caring deeply about those churches of brother Christians in other communities. In every case their one authority was Christ, and their one method for seeking the will of Christ was meeting together in prayer and discussion, to discover that will.

The gathered church would testify to the whole church that

the power of the Spirit is real not only in personal lives, but also in the life of congregations.

The Gathered Church as a Vehicle of the Spirit

The belief of the free churches of the gathered tradition is that it is in fact possible for a congregation of God's people to live faithfully under the sole authority of the Holy Spirit—and that it is possible for such congregations to live without any other human authority.

They are well aware that theirs is the most dangerous of church traditions. But they also believe it is one of the most exciting of church traditions. They believe it contains within its life much of what modern man is most eagerly looking for in church life: true democracy, a seeking, pilgrim spirit, an equal, even exalted place for the layman, the necessity of an attitude of humble devotion, and most particularly, an authentic new authority.

The church today is looking for a new authority. Many Christians are obviously restive under an overweening authority of men. And surely the "ecumenical movement" among Protestants is looking for some basis of authority under which all Christians can live.

Why not the most obvious and greatest authority of all? Why not the undiluted, dangerous, but exhilarating authority of the direct rule of Christ himself?

This is why the free churches, whether they know it or not, have an answer to the ecumenical dilemma. They have, often unconsciously, preserved, at least in ideal, a way of church life that gives Christ's Holy Spirit the opportunity to work through the whole life of the whole people. Not that they created it or completely possess it, but that they have tried to live with it and make it their way.

Is not this the sort of life, reduced to its simplest elements, that the whole church is seeking to find? I suspect that the

The Spirit's Power 131

gathered churches have been as afraid of the Holy Spirit as anyone. I am sure that they have often been unworthy witnesses to the power of the Spirit. But at least, if the whole church is agreed that it is the Spirit that it needs, then the gathered churches have the opportunity to call the church back to a new life in the Spirit. Now, at least, they have a chance to recover that power in their own churches, and to have something to offer when their friends from all the traditions of Christendom come looking for a new way for all Christians to live in the unity of the Spirit.

Our task is to open up the way for the Holy Spirit to live again in the churches. Our task is to teach all Christ's own people that they are part of his plan for leading the church into unity: that he needs each one, and can use them, and give them power. Our task is to show the world that the church, wherever it is found, is essentially those people in that place who have covenanted together to obey Christ and then to bear each other's burdens. Our task is to be instruments for the renewing and reuniting of the church in our day.

The witness of the gathered church to the power of the Holy Spirit is that the church—wherever it is, whether in Lambeth Palace, or Vatican City, or Main Street America—is the people's church, not the priest's church, that it is Christ's church, not the hierarchy's church. And its witness is that the people, powered by their Lord, can do in homes and shops, in offices and schools, what the theologians and the professors, the bishops and executives have never been quite sure they *could* do.

The kind of church the gathered church would propose, then, is a church in which all the people share and in which every person counts.

And it would propose that the whole church be made up of churches centering their lives on the Spirit.

Every church would like to think it already has the Spirit in its life. We would all be glad to claim the Spirit as our motive and our mover.

But humbly, I hope, the free churches would make a special claim to be churches of the Spirit.

Every church tradition has some system of authority, some way in which duty is done, and claims are made, and authority is exercised. Some churches gain their authority through a theory of apostolic succession exercised through the office of bishop. Others exercise certain authority over local churches and people through the guidance of a democratically elected presbytery. Others do so through synods or superintendents.

But the gathered church has none of these—no book of index, no presbytery, no bishop. Each one of these, in its own tradition, helps to keep local churches straight. But in the conception of the gathered church there is only one authority, and before his no human authorities can exist. That authority is Christ's: what the English Congregationalists are fond of calling "the Crown Rights of the Redeemer." The Redeemer alone has the right to rule. And he rules directly and specifically without any intermediary. He will tell his church what it must do. He will guide it where it must go. He will warn it when it has wandered astray.

He does it through the instrument of the "Church Meeting." When the people meet in faith he is there as he promised to be, and he guides them as he promised he would. He does it through his Spirit. He touches the heart of his people when they pray. He guides their thinking as they talk and discuss. He opens possibilities to them as they think together. He is there, directly, personally, powerfully in his Spirit.

And it does something to you if you are part of such a people. You suddenly bear responsibilities which not all Christians feel called to bear. You suddenly are dealing with concerns you never had thought would be yours. You suddenly have to listen, and pray, and be sensitive as you never had to do before. And you begin to become a pilgrim in a way you

The Spirit's Power

had not done before. You begin to be more open in a way you often were not before. Christ's Spirit is somehow real as often he was not before.

It is on the basis of this instrument of church government, this way of church life that the gathered church would make its claim to offer a way of the Spirit.

Finally, the gathered church would claim to offer the whole church a freedom to follow Christ. Of course, it is this freedom in the gathered churches that is most misunderstood. "Where is your discipline?" people ask. "Where is your common heritage, your great tradition, your common characteristics from one church to another? You're just a bunch of anarchists with every man for himself!"

—It could so easily be that way. In the times when the gathered church fails, when it falls short of its calling, it is that way. But at its best it is far from that. At its best its discipline is as direct and sure as any, because it is Christ's discipline, and his direction.

"But are not other churches under the rule of Christ?" the inquirer asks. Yes—but they have added safeguards, protective clauses. Not so the gathered church. It has Christ for its guide and stay, Christ—and that is all. We have burned our bridges behind us. It is discover Christ's will and do it—or perish! And some churches have perished. They needed a help. They did not seek and no help came.

That is why this is a dangerous way. That is why freedom in anybody's hands is a risk. What if you do your own will and not Christ's? What if you believe just anything you want, and not the gospel? It can happen. That is why some say that the way of the gathered church is just too hot to handle.

Yet this freedom was never demanded for anarchy. It was never demanded for the sake of discipleship without discipline.

And so, about the freedom of the gathered church there is something quite exciting. It is creative as not all church life is. It is fast-moving and free-wheeling as not all church life is, because it is just you and your Lord: just this one congregation waiting to hear Christ's words for their life. You have to listen if you are going to hear, you have to pray if you are going to know. Everyone has to listen, and everyone has to pray, because it is the people who make the decisions. And the future depends upon them. Progress waits upon them.

So a gathered church has responsibilities few churches have —and a privilege few churches have. Its life is dangerous. It is full of pitfalls. But it is exciting as any life can be. It has opportunities that few other lives offer. It has a power for reconciliation that few churches have, because it is a church free to follow Christ.

No Gathered Church, No Unity

Can there conceivably be here, then, a basis on which Christians might come together?—a basis, fresh and new and yet old as the church itself, which would be free of the major stumbling blocks of the past, and yet inclusive of the most vital elements in the day-to-day local life of every church in every major denominational tradition? Could there possibly be a way left, as yet untried, that would preserve the uniqueness, the ethos of each church's local life without compromising anyone's personal integrity or most precious principles? A way which would uphold no doctrine of authority offensive to some, but rather an authority of Christ himself acceptable to all?

This is a question not seriously asked in ecumenical circles, at least a question not seriously considered if it is asked, because it seems too impossible. What way could there possibly be that could exalt the principles basic to every Christian tradition without being a hopeless potpourri of principles impossible to reconcile, or a compromise so watered down and weak as to be without meaning for anyone? That is a counsel of perfection that few statesmen of the church would want to

The Spirit's Power

give for fear of being laughed out of court as hopelessly naïve and idealistic.

Nevertheless, is there such a way? Beyond all the compromises of reordinations, and episcopal prerogatives, and closed communion, and the claims of "true" churches or incompleteness of "compromise" churches, is there a way to recognition of a basic integrity and wholeness of all Christian churches that could provide a new respect for the uniqueness of all traditions and a way of preserving and sharing this uniqueness for us all?

There is a way, I think, by going at the ecumenical movement from a completely new direction—from the direction of its "low" side, rather than from its "high" side. It is just conceivable that in looking at the ecumenical movement from this perspective, we might discover that the "low" churches have something very "high" about them and that the "free" side has something very "authoritative" in its life.

What I would make bold to suggest here is a new look at the church, and the consideration by those who care, of a new basis for Christian unity. I think it could help to provide the new appreciation for each other about which we have all been talking, as well as an alternative plan toward that new unity in the church for which we all are seeking.

I would unashamedly ask here for a reconsideration, among ecumenical leaders and among the hosts of those who are concerned, of the principles of free churchmanship which have within them the seeds, at least, of a life common to all our traditions.

If the church is to live anywhere, if it is to become a reality anywhere, it must become a reality and live at the local level. There is no real church without somewhere, at some point, the gathered church—the church which Christ has gathered together in one place to live for him and to be faithful to him.

If the emphasis can be put on the power of the church at this local level to be really the church, really to be used by the Spirit of Christ, and if all the various traditions could center their thinking and conversation upon this vital level of the church's life, they would find, I am convinced, an increasing sense of unity, an increasing awareness of common heritage, an increasing excitement about the vast possibilities of a church united in heart and spirit at this level of day-to-day life.

The genius of such a view of the church is that a truly "Spirit church" becomes inevitably a reconciling church, in its internal life and in its life in the world; and as a reconciling church it can be nothing but a unifying and united church.

The key is the Spirit, and the willingness of all the churches and denominations to look to the Spirit as the heart and the hope of their new life. And the gathered church could make it possible.

8

A Church for the World

As this book is written, a new day has come for the church in America and the church in the world. Imperceptibly and inevitably it has come, a day when something new is demanded. Curiously, that demand is made because now its fulfillment seems possible.

The world has come to expect something from the church which for decades it has not expected. It looks for leadership from the church, it looks for strength, it looks for integrity, it looks for life from the church. It looks for an excitement, and a relevance, and an importance that will make the church a force to be taken seriously, a spiritual power to be honored, an institution vital for national life.

The experimental ministries of Protestantism and the winds of renewal in Roman Catholicism have convinced the world it can happen. There must be a new church: a more faithful church, a more loving church, a more powerful church, a more sacrificing church, a greater church. There must be a freer church, a more open church, a simpler church, a more united church, a more Christlike church. There must be no longer a church for itself, a church for the church. There must be a church for the world, a missionary church, a reconciling and uniting church, a transforming church, a church that will change the world!

The question is, when will the church allow itself to be such a church? How can such a church be fashioned? And what form of church will it be? What would a church fashioned to face these times, and this world, be like?

The purpose of this concluding chapter is to suggest finally a plan for such a church.

The Hope in the World

The hunger is in many hearts. The concern is shared by many people in many different traditions of the church that, as Jesus said, "They all may be one; as thou, Father, art in me, and I in Thee, that they also may be one in us." This is the longing: the longing that Christians who love the same Lord, that men of the Cross who fight under the same banner, that servants of the Saviour who are healing the hurts and binding up the wounds of the world with the same love should not have to be at enmity with each other, should not have to peer at each other across walls of misunderstanding and fear, and should not have to exclude each other at the table of the Lord, nor deny each other's call and ministry. If this longing is real at all, there is indeed hope for unity in the church.

How Can the Walls Come Down?

But how? How will it ever come? How will we ever tear down those barriers between, and still maintain our integrity, still be true to the witness we believe God has given us? Can we just tear them down with our hands as Cardinal Cushing of Boston has said he would like to do? In a pluralistic society such as ours, in a land where two hundred sixty-seven denominations make up the Christian church with each laying claim to some uniqueness from New Testament Christianity, can

A Church for the World

anyone seriously suggest that "they may be one" is even the most remote of possibilities?

So far as I am aware, nobody knows. If "one church" means one great, overarching, all-powerful organization, marshaling twenty million people into even lines with the same kinds of churches, the same forms of worship, the same dress and ritual, the same creeds and confessions—in short, one vast Protestant church facing one vast Roman Catholic church, or even one great structure including Roman Catholics and Orthodox, and Protestants, with the same tight control and obvious similarity and regimentation that the Roman Church exhibits today—then I doubt very much if there are many who would want it.

It is interesting that even today, for all the groundswell toward one great church, there is, especially among the younger generation of ecumenical enthusiasts, a certain disenchantment with large organization as seen in the World Council of Churches.

A prominent Protestant leader, Bishop Gerald Kennedy, writing in response to the Blake-Pike proposal for a Catholic and Reformed Church in America, expresses a very similar concern when he writes:

> The World Council has some members [who] . . . see the real goal as one church with one organization and they press forward bravely toward that union. These have their counterparts in the National Council of Churches, and there are among us those who think that to stop short of one organization is betrayal.
>
> On the other hand, there are those who oppose this goal vehemently, among whom I find myself.[1]

A united Christianity needs some kind of organization. For common mission and outreach there may need to be some

---

[1] *The Challenge to Reunion*, Edited by Robert McGraw Brown and David H. Short. McGraw-Hill Book Company, Inc., New York, 1963, p. 224. Chapter, "The Problem of Church Unity," Gerald Kennedy.

forms for working together and combining efforts. But there are at least some among the church leaders themselves who look for a church bound together in other ways, drawing power from other sources, winning the world by other means.

What Laymen Are Looking For

If one were to canvass the lay people who are the church in America, one might discover that the forms and trappings of great organization are not at all what they are thinking of when they speak about the "one church." They have dreamed a dream, too. They have shared a hope, too. They also have a hunger in their hearts. And I suspect it has much more to do with the neighbor next door who is a Christian of a denomination not familiar to most, or the church across town whose tradition is different, than it does with forming an organization somewhere, some day that will make us all the same and blot out all our differences.

I think they want to talk with that friend about faith without fighting. I think they want to visit his church and worship there without feeling inferior or superior. I think they want to welcome that friend to their church and have the invitation accepted, to see their own minister and their friend's pastor or priest working together as friends, to labor themselves with Roman Catholics and Orthodox, Southern Baptists and Episcopalians, in the same cause as friends of the Master. I think their dream is of a changed relationship where the ecumenical leaders say repeatedly that they want it too—at the local level in the church where they worship, in the town where they live, among the friends whom they know.

The true church for me will be one where Baptists can be Baptists, and Catholics can be Catholics, and Episcopalians can be Episcopalians, but will respect each other's gifts, and share a mutual ministry, and labor in common tasks as one

A Church for the World

people of one Lord, proclaiming the one gospel that is Good News to us all.

I do not mean the church cannot be one. I do not even mean it can have no organization. I only mean that what I long for as a parish parson, and what I think hundreds of lay people long for as the body of the church, is a new relationship where they live—a new relationship that would mean a difference in their town, and in everybody's town across the world.

Many things would have to be agreed upon. Some differences would have to be decided, and some settlements would have to be made. But not all. Even some patterns within the life of individual local churches would change. But not all.

For something that often does not have a chance now could do its work then, and that is love. In my own family we have differences that are very great. My father is a Congregational minister. But of his children only one remains a Congregationalist. One daughter lives in Germany, a member of the Reformed Church of the Netherlands. Another teaches school in New York City, and is a devout and faithful "low" Episcopalian. One son, married to an Episcopalian, is a minister and a theological lecturer in the United Church of South India. One son remains who is a Congregationalist and a minister in that tradition. And we by no means agree on our theology nor on our doctrine of the church. Between the generations deep differences exist: deeper ones, I suspect, than those among the children, although there are differences there as well. And yet we are still a family, and we still are fellow Christians, and we still respect each other's gifts and traditions, and often we exercise a mutual ministry, because between us there is love. The church as it should be will have love like that.

Some Ways of Organizing the Great Church Coming

But still the question comes to "how?" To be sure, we must feel our way. To be sure, no one really knows. To be sure, we must have faith and follow on where only God can lead.

But questionable assumptions have been already made. The Blake-Pike proposal for a Catholic and Reformed Church in America is an example of such an assumption. Certain forms and ministries in this proposed step toward the "coming great church" are assumed, without any question, nor with any recognition of how hard it would be for thousands of Christians in the great denominational traditions of America to take. Blake said in his famous sermon,

> I propose that without adopting any particular theory of historic succession, the reunited church shall provide at its inception for the consecration of all its bishops by bishops and presbyters both in the apostolic succession and out of it . . .

Is the great church ahead to have bishops and a theory of apostolic succession? Must it have bishops and the kind of questionable doctrine of authority which is such an offense to so many Christians, particularly of the evangelical and reformed wings of the church? This is not to mention the office of Presbyter and ordained ruling elder which he goes on to say the Presbyterians would contribute to the reunited church. This itself makes assumptions that cannot be fairly made in view of the free-church background of the fourth denomination invited which has neither of these traditions.

But take just episcopacy alone. In all the current conversations about the ecumenical movement and the "great church" for which men are planning, always the tacit assumption is made that episcopacy will be part of it—and indeed, one very particular theory of episcopacy based on an apostolic succession physically transmitted through the ages from an apostle

A Church for the World

who, on very thin grounds, is claimed to be the original bishop of Rome.

And yet this is one of the greatest of all ecumenical stumbling blocks today—standing in the way both of a mutually recognized and shared ministry and of freedom for all Christians to draw near to the Lord's table. Understood in this way it is difficult to see how it can possibly be accepted by the hosts of other Christians.

Even an Episcopalian as prominent in the ecumenical movement as Canon T. O. Wedel of the Washington Cathedral writes:

> But unless a view of episcopal church order can extricate itself from this Roman dogma of a vicarial Apostolic succession and priesthood, its rejection by evangelical Christendom is foreordained. This theory of the ministry a Biblical Protestantism will never accept. The doctrine of Apostolic Succession as a vicarial ministry must go.[2]

Here, an Episcopal leader himself questions whether such a view of the ministry, with its direct bearing both on "orders" and upon "sacrament," can possibly become the basis of a reunited church. Many other Protestants would echo his sentiments. Perhaps even Bishop Pike and Dr. Blake would agree with him.

Why then should this be assumed to be the only possible basis of unity? Are there not other ways also valid, other ways which might also point a road toward a reunited church, other ways which might contain within them the genius of including most of the elements basic to the day-to-day life of all traditions in the Christian church?

The thesis of this book is that such another way does exist, and that it is one which comes out of and is suggested, at least, by the life of the free churches. Before the ecumenical die is

---

[2] "The Coming Great Church," quoted by Gerald Kennedy in *The Challenge to Reunion, op. cit.*, p. 227.

cast this book would plead that the genius of the free churches be at least considered as a path to Christian unity.

Removing the Stumbling Blocks

Winfred E. Garrison, one of the leaders of the ecumenical movement, has made a long list of those principles of Christian Church life which could be stumbling blocks to other Christians in a reunited church:

> ... the primacy and infallibility of the bishop of Rome, or the Eastern Orthodox liturgy, or the historic episcopate, or the presbyterial polity, or congregational independency, or immersion, or the real presence of Christ's Body in the Eucharist, or the trinitarian formula of the Nicene Creed.[3]

These constitute most of the distinctive features in the church today. But among them is one which, among Protestants at least, has been a most difficult principle to reconcile with the humility of our Lord himself and with the gospel of love which he proclaimed and lived. That is the principle of the historic episcopate, the doctrine of apostolic succession maintained through history, presumably by a physical laying on of hands from one bishop to another, beginning with the apostle Peter. Reference has already been made to this problem.

Many Protestants, of course, find it difficult to take seriously any claim that Peter ever was, in fact, the bishop of Rome, or that a physical line through twenty centuries has been maintained without break. "Most Methodists," according to Bishop Kennedy of that church, "would accept John Wesley's summing up: 'I never could see it proved; and I am persuaded I never shall.' "[4]

---

[3] *The Quest and Character of A United Church*, Abingdon Press, Nashville, p. 217, quoted by Gerald Kennedy in *The Challenge to Reunion, op. cit.*, p. 227.
[4] *Journal*, Feb. 19, 1761.

A Church for the World 145

The problem for Protestants is not really whether the theory is historically valid or not, but the problem of what the doctrine—once it is held to and believed by a denomination such as the Episcopal church—does to relations among Christians of differing traditions. Many churches have principles precious to them, but rarely are they used to exclude other Christians from their worship, or to demean the validity of the ministry in other traditions, or to make judgments on the faith of other Christians.

The problem centers in what the church calls "orders" and "communion." "Orders" has to do with the proper ordination of men to the ministry. It is the conviction of those who accept the doctrine of apostolic succession through the historic episcopate that no man is fully ordained to the Christian ministry until he receives the laying on of hands in ordination from a bishop who has been himself properly consecrated. While the Anglican Communion in its *Appeal to All Christian People* at the Lambeth Conference in 1920 acknowledged that the ministry in other Christian traditions "has been manifestly blessed and owned by the Holy Spirit as effective means of Grace" it nevertheless insists, in all its Christian Unity conversations, on a form of service at the time of uniting with any such denomination, which is in fact reordination of those ministers who may long have been already properly ordained ministers in their own traditions. In the United Church of South India, where certain candidates were ordained as bishops and all future ministers of the church are episcopally ordained by them, it comes down to this. In the Ceylon and North India plans where all the ministers of the uniting denominations kneel and receive the laying on of hands from the newly consecrated bishops, it comes down to this. And in the proposed service of mutual reciprocal laying on of hands in the future merger of the Anglican and Methodist churches of England, it comes down to this: reordination.

And yet are ministers of the evangelical traditions, who

received ordination to the gospel ministry by the laying on of hands of their brethren and fathers in the ministry in a continuing, historic apostolic succession of faith to deny the validity of that ordination and of all those years of ministry by submitting all over again to an ordination required of them for the sake of maintaining one denomination's particular and narrow view of the ministry? I know very few ministers in the evangelical tradition of Protestanism whose consciences would permit them to submit to this!

But beyond this the theory of apostolic succession through a physical line of bishops has put up bars around the communion table. Whereas Jesus says: "Come unto me, all ye that labor and are heavy laden," the churches accepting the historic episcopate say, "Come unto me only ye who are confirmed in our tradition." While some individual parish priests in the episcopal tradition do in fact welcome all Christians to receive communion, it is nevertheless understood as standard practice in the Anglican Communion that this sacrament is to be reserved for those who have been properly confirmed—that is, confirmed in the Anglican communion by a properly consecrated bishop of that church.

The assumption here is that no communion service can be valid unless the ordination of the man conducting the service is valid; i.e., unless he has been ordained in the ministry of the apostolic succession. For the member of a church in this tradition in America this means not only that a question is raised about whether his Congregational, or Baptist, or Presbyterian friend is really welcome to receive communion in his church, but also that an even greater question is raised as to whether he can receive communion in his friend's church at the hands of a Baptist, Presbyterian, or Congregational minister. Certainly such a minister would not be welcome to conduct a service of the Lord's Supper in an Episcopal church!

Can Christians so exclude each other at these most vital points in the church's life and ever expect to grow in Christian unity? Unity in the church will depend upon finding a way around, over, or through these major stumbling blocks.

A New Way for the Church to Try

And yet the changes in attitude hold out hope that something of significance may happen to help us find our way together. At least, the new winds blowing through the church and the quickening eagerness everywhere encourage Christians in every quarter to search our own hearts and our own traditions to see what it is we have that is unique and worthy that might be brought as a gift to the whole church.

It has been my growing conviction that the way out of which all the free churches have come holds within its life something unique and profound that has been largely overlooked by ecumenical leaders. The reason it has been overlooked is that too often it has been only a potential and not an actual part of our life. Free churches like other churches have unwittingly submitted to some of the sins of our day. We have not always understood what our own uniqueness was.

But even though in modern times we have forsaken it, the genius is there: the way of life is waiting to be reclaimed not only by our churches, but by the whole church. Many characteristics of the free churches are qualities every church would claim, principles of life to which every church would cry "Amen!" The difference is only that often they are more radically lived and more seriously taken among the free churches.

Take the dependence upon the Holy Spirit for guidance and direction, and power and life. Every Christian and every church would claim this as his dependence, too. And yet who makes his dependence so radical as do the free churches in their dependence on him in every act of worship, or in their dependence on his guidance when they gather in "Church Meeting" to make decisions?

Or who would not claim to seek the Word of God in worship, and yet who exalts it more than those churches that honor the place of preaching, and come each Sunday sincerely expecting to hear God's Word in the preaching of the sermon?

Or what about the place of the laity in the church? Everybody is talking about how important the laymen are. But who has taken them so seriously for so long as have the free churches who have given all the people in every church the right to make that church's decisions in common meeting together, and who have permitted them, by vote of the people, to administer the sacraments, and to preach?

Even the Anglican Church in its Article 19 of the 39 Articles states:

> The visible church of Christ is a *congregation* (italics mine) of faithful men, in which the pure Word of God is preached, and the sacraments be duly ministered according to Christ's ordinance, in all those things that of necessity are requisite to the same.

And yet who seeks more radically to live that conviction than the free churches which recognize the local congregation as "the church" and claim for it the right to be free and autonomous before men so that it may be obedient to the will and leading of Christ?

Not a Christian or a church is unaware of Jesus' ministry to the lost and the poor of the world, and of his welcome to all men to "come unto me." And yet what church traditions take him more seriously than those who reclaim the Lord's table for the Lord, and invite all to come to it who love him, and who believe themselves called? The "free table" is a cherished heritage of the "free churches" and is one of the gifts they would most eagerly bring to a reunited church: that, and a free life under Christ, a life free in the regular meeting of the whole people to follow the lead of the Lord.

It is exciting to see in our own day the way in which other

A Church for the World

branches of the church are rediscovering in their own life these gifts which the free churches are dedicated to continuing. Canon Southcott in his industrial parish in Leeds hitting upon the gathering of his whole people together and letting them make the church's decisions in obedience to the Spirit's guidance is one exciting break-through from the Anglican side. Obviously, he has discovered what English Congregationalists long have called "The Church Meeting." To see him, in the little documentary film "Alf Goes to Work," conducting baptisms in the center of the church at the heart of public worship would warm the hearts of his free church brethren who long have held baptism to be a gospel sacrament to be celebrated not privately, but in the midst of the great congregation. Not least of the rediscoveries taking place on the "episcopal" side of the church's life is the new emphasis upon the importance of laymen in even the Catholic Church. Wrote Boston's Cardinal Cushing in his pastoral letter in the spring of 1963,

> Because of his more intimate engagement in the world, the layman is likely to bring insights and understanding which only such an essential involvement can provide; the teaching authorities, in the church must accept this competence where it exists and rejoice in the opportunities for good it offers for their guidance.

These are signs, I would humbly submit, that at the level of the renewal of the church's basic daily life a rediscovery is being made of principles of churchmanship, which have long been preserved in the free churches. It is in this atmosphere of mutual discovery and open listening on the part of all Christians that this book has set out to present in love and hope what I believe to be some of the great gifts that the gathered church has to give in our day to the reunited church.

The Congregation as a Key to the Reunited Church

The heart of the free church doctrine of what is a church is the belief that it is fully formed in the congregation, in the gathered group of people whom Christ has called, if they are faithful to his guidance in their midst.

This is not by any means to say that nothing is needed beyond the local church. The traditions that give autonomy to local churches also have mission boards, and societies, and even district ministers or superintendents who can have a care for local churches and be a help to them, especially in extending their ministry. The free churches are not narrow and parochial in their view of the church. Historically, in America, they have been among the first to recognize and meet the need for mission, service, education, and involvement beyond the local parish. They produced America's first Foreign Missions Board, her first Home Mission Board, her first Bible society, her first college, and the first higher education for Negroes. Free churchmen have historically been in the vanguard of the abolition, women's suffrage, and more recent social action movements.

It would be unfair of me to represent the Baptist, Disciples of Christ, Covenant, Pentecostal, United Church of Christ, Congregational, Evangelical Free Church, Advent Christian, Assemblies of God, and other free church traditions as being radical "congregationalists" in their view of the local church. All these traditions have high regard and reserve a special place in their heart and life for "the fellowship." Local congregations do depend on each other for encouragement and counsel. All have assemblies that gather together periodically on a national, state, and county or city basis to share mutual concerns and to inspire and help each other. The life of the "whole" church, the "universal" church, the "great cloud of witnesses" of the church militant upon earth and triumphant

A Church for the World

in heaven is very real to them. They feel themselves very much a part of the "great church" in this sense.

The local gathered church I know best is far more ecumenical than it is independent. Its staff is made up of persons representing five different denominations. It cooperates fully with both Roman Catholic and Protestant churches in its town, contributes substantially to two different missionary societies of its tradition, has cooperated in establishing an interracial inner city nursery school with a church of another denomination, and has founded a Group Home for Delinquent Girls in cooperation with a social agency and the state government.

But when it comes to the question of who has authority in the church, their claim is for Christ alone as head of the church. By no means do they believe that the local, gathered church is all there is of the church! What they *do* say is that if Christ is truly present with the two or three gathered together, then he is the fullness of ecclesiastical authority himself, and nothing more is needed that is more authoritative, or more official, or more regular. Bishops and Councils may give wise Christian advice that perhaps ought to be accepted and followed by local churches. But the only authority that can commend that counsel to the local church is the authority of the Holy Spirit himself, commending it directly to that church.

A local church is like gold. It is not all the gold in the world. But it is as truly gold as any other gold, even though its amount may be very small. The fullness of the local church's authority is determined by the fullness of Christ's presence *in* that church, and that people's acknowledgment of and obedience to his power.

Just as this freedom to follow the Holy Spirit in the local situation is the great strength of the gathered church, so is its great weakness that a hard-hearted, disobedient people can refuse to follow the Holy Spirit in its midst and can be overcome by the devil himself in terrible acts of prejudice and self-serving. The way of the free churches has no guarantees against human weakness and error. It is a very dangerous way, full of great risks. But it is also a very exciting and potentially very powerful way.

And the uniqueness of it today is that it embodies a form of life—the gathered church—which is common and basic to every Christian tradition. Everybody has it and both free churchmen and high churchmen are beginning to realize that it is still the front line of the church. A concept not only of church life but of the very doctrine of authority in the church is opened up here with the realization that from two vastly different positions we are being led to it, and are finding it good.

Surely the recovered and recovering emphasis in the Catholic Church on the importance of the laity represents a democratizing trend in that church which cannot help but open up the thinking of that clerically dominated church to the life in the free churches where lay persons are accorded full freedom not only to speak out, but to lead and to act with authority in our church's life. This, it seems to me, will inevitably move certain decision-making powers back to the level of the local church, and indeed exalt the life of the local church to a new importance which it has not always had in the more authoritarian churches.

In fact, any movement—especially a liturgical movement—back across the medieval years of its greatest splendor and authority to its simpler and more creative years of the first century cannot help but uncover, not only an emphasis upon the simplicity of worship and the people's place in it, but a corresponding emphasis also upon the vitality of the local fellowship of Christians, their importance as a company of committed people, and upon the real and most relevant nature of the church as a gathered church: a church made up of people gathered together by the call of Christ in local particular places such as Rome, or Thessalonica, or Antioch, or Jerusalem. Here "The Church" was the church in Rome, or the church in Ephesus, and the vitality of its world witness depended upon the vitality of its particular witness in a given town or city.

To come alive at the local level, at the grass roots, can mean nothing but a re-emphasis upon the local church, and a recognition that if the church is to live anywhere it must live here, and be vital here, and powerful here, and affect human lives here. The wave of the future, in the progress of Christian unity, I am sure will be a re-emphasis upon and a new appreciation of the local church.

In the light of this, to have standing in the wings a group of church traditions long accustomed to emphasis upon the importance and witness of local churches and to giving birth to local churches of free and imaginative and creative character will make opportunity for a new meeting ground for the diverse traditions of the world's churches.

The Congregation as Meeting Ground and Battle Ground

If there is to be a reunited church anywhere there must be a gathered church somewhere. There is no unity, there is not one church, unless it exists where the church lives, where the church worships, where the church works, and mounts its mission. There is no unity, then, unless there is unity in the local church—in the church where God's people are physically gathered. It is the glory and the joy of the gathered churches that they can offer such a way. They can offer it because they embody it.

As long ago as 1865, the churches of the Congregational way sensed the special contribution they had to make to Christian unity and reconciliation. In the "Proceedings" of the National Council of the Congregational Churches in that year, this is what they said to each other and to the world:

> It is the just glory of our churches that they are of all churches the most truly catholic, . . . we have placed vital Christianity, the renewing and saving power of the Gospel and the cross, first and highest in our religious system, and have made modes of worship and forms of administration subordinate to life.

In the Declaration of Faith of that Council they go on to say:

> We hold it to be a distinctive excellence of our Congregational system, that it exalts that which is more, above that which is less important, and, by the simplicity of its organization, facilitates, in communities where the population is limited, the union of all true believers in one Christian church; and that the division of such communities into several weak and jealous societies holding the same common faith, is a sin against the unity of the body of Christ, and at once the shame and scandal of Christendom.

Obviously, these men held a high view of the church and they disparaged division and jealousy among local churches as much as we, but they deeply believed that in their free system Christ had given them a uniting "way" for the whole church. They go on:

> We rejoice that, through the influence of our free system of apostolic order, we can hold fellowship with all who acknowledge Christ and act efficiently in the work of restoring unity to the divided church and of bringing back harmony and peace, among all "who love the Lord Jesus Christ in sincerity."
>
> Thus recognizing the unity of the church of Christ in all the world, and knowing that we are but one branch of Christ's people, while adhering to our own peculiar faith and order, we extend to all believers the hand of Christian fellowship upon the basis of those great fundamental truths in which all Christians should agree. . . .
>
> We believe also in the organized and visible church, in the

A Church for the World

ministry of the Word, in the sacraments of Baptism and the Lord's Supper, in the resurrection of the body, and in the final judgment. . . .

Affirming now our belief that those who thus hold "one faith, one Lord, one baptism," together constitute one Catholic Church, the several households of which though called by different names, are one body of Christ; and that these members of His body are sacredly bound to keep "the unity of the Spirit in the bond of peace, "we declare that we will cooperate with all who hold these truths. With them we will carry the Gospel into every part of this land, and with them we will go into all the world, and "preach the gospel to every creature."

Here was a form of church life reduced to its basic faith and basic life, set upon the divine errand of mission and bravely offered to the whole church as a way toward the finding of a real Christian unity. It is out of such vision as this that, a hundred years later, the gathered churches of the world have an opportunity to offer the same hope of unity in the whole church for which we all seek, and to offer the following plan.

A Church for the World

A church for the world of our day must be above all else *a missionary church*. It must be a church on the move, a church reaching out, winning the world, healing its heart, and bringing it hope.

It must be *a simple church*. It must offer the world the heart of the faith, the basic foundation of its life, and not all the paraphernalia of doctrine and dress, which are not essential.

It must be *a local church*. It must be a church whose reality can be seen and witnessed in every community—a unity of Christians working together and worshiping together and living together.

It must be *a loving church*. It must be a church in which love is so real that in faith and love the Lord's Supper can be shared, baptism can be shared, the preaching of the Word can be shared, fellowship can be shared, and Christian mission can be shared.

It must be *a church of the Spirit*, and not of mechanics. Its reality must not be primarily of organization, but rather of Spirit. It must be a unity real because of the freedom it gives the heart, and not false because of a machinery that binds the body and the mind.

It must be *a church of Christ*—a church embodying his forgiving, personal, unorthodox spirit of letting love make the difference.

It must be a free-moving, creative church, willing to try new things, willing to sacrifice prestige and power and even life to be true to its Lord and his concern for the world and for little people. It must have the freedom to try new things, to start an East Harlem Protestant Parish or an Iona Community or a coffee house or any of the rest without hierarchical veto, but with support and help from the fellowship.

A church for the world must maintain the identity of great and varied traditions within the whole church. It must allow them to live, for the sake of variety and human need, but also to preserve creative tension.

Its basis of unity must be spiritually binding but not legally binding. Its discipline must be love's discipline, and its care and oversight must be purely pastoral care and loving oversight.

Its very freedom should make common mission possible, and its love and humble recognition of the validity of others' faith and life should make possible common worship—common coming to the table, the common blessing of baptism, and the common speaking and hearing of the Word.

The following "Proposal for Christian Unity" is made, therefore, to be true to these principles. Out of the long ex-

A Church for the World

perience of the gathered principle the free churches propose as a way of bringing a concrete working Christian unity:

1. That there be an agreed acceptance that the local church, when true to Jesus' injunction, constitutes equal authority in the church with other parts of the church. That it is fully the church, even though it is not the whole of the church. This would mean an acceptance of the congregation as the basic unit and means of life of the whole church.
2. That there be an acceptance of mutual orders of the ministry. That the apostolic succession of faith and spirit and the laying on of hands of all God's people (through deacons and brother ministers) be accepted as valid for service in the sanctuary for administering the two basic sacraments, and for the preaching of the Word, and the leading of the people.
3. That baptism be formally agreed upon as a universal sacrament and that the Lord's Supper be likewise accepted as a common sacrament binding all Christians together and therefore to be recognized as valid in every church as long as instituted by the words of Jesus and carried out by congregation and minister faithfully in his Spirit.
4. That it be agreed that denominations as such remain intact, but conceive it their task to serve and support the local churches of their tradition. That denominations—in mission especially—seek to engage in ministries together.
    a. That denominations seek in every way possible to reduce their administrative functions and other operations, so as to save money for the common cause and to put back into service in actual situations of ministry ordained clergy and lay persons who had been taken out of service for denominational work.
5. That agreement on a simple covenant be reached and denominations and local churches enter into covenant agreements with each other "to walk together in the ways of the Lord" in every area of life that they now can, and that they will be able in future to do.
    a. That local churches individually enter into such covenants

of mutual mission and ministry, particularly at the community level and the neighborhood level.
  b. That these covenants be undertaken among churches with the purpose of doing as much together now as they can, and being free to do more together later as progress is made.
  c. That this new relationship be symbolized by Boards of Deacons or other lay officers becoming automatic planning boards in communities, meeting together for community or neighborhood strategy in mission.
  d. That a "covenant of common discipleship" be the binding agreement which will unite local Christians spiritually, but leave them free to maintain their former heritage. That the emphasis of the covenant be on common faith, common mission, and common worship.
6. That the ministers in local towns or cities come together at regular intervals for common spiritual discipline and study, leading to a renewal of the ministers' lives as well as the congregations'.
7. That each denomination agree to send a pastoral letter to all its churches suggesting such local plans of action.
8. And that to begin the new covenant relationship between local churches a "Scripture service" of praise be held by all the participating churches in a central auditorium on a Sunday evening, looking forward to their work and worship together. That common communion services between Protestant churches be held as soon as such are possible.

This proposal does not attempt to change denominational labels and loyalty. It does not attempt to change or break up locally worshiping congregations. It does not attempt to change basic doctrines or dogmas.

It does, however, offer the free and open basis of a covenant relationship in which Christian friendship, Christian mission, and Christian worship can be carried on. It is only a beginning, but it *is* a beginning.

Its key is a personal relationship built upon Christian friendship and prayer among churchmen lay and clerical in neighborhoods and towns. It is, I think, something more than councils of churches do, even though it would appear much simpler and less structured. Where it can grow is out of earnest prayer and growing friendship among ministers and other Christians in the community where they live and work. It can grow there because men know each other there, and come to trust each other there, and find the Holy Spirit in each other's lives and ministries there.

We have discussed a great deal. Here is a way to begin. Here is a way not only for ecumenically minded Protestants to begin. Here is a way for Catholics to begin, and evangelicals and other churchmen to begin. Here is a way, particularly, for those Christians who have never felt part of the ecumenical movement to begin.

It is a way to put aside old prejudices, to eschew the old clichés, to say never again the bitter words, but to begin to take a new look, to try a fresh start, to see fellow Christians not as Catholics or Congregationalists, Brethren or Baptists, Episcopalians or Pentecostalists, but to see them as they were when the Church was new: "friends" of the Way.

Here, I think, is a way to see the world church, and to see it whole: to see it where it lives, where it has most in common, where people face each other and face the Lord most concretely, most personally, and most powerfully—in congregations; in gathered companies of Christian people.

It seems almost too simple to be different, to be too obvious not to have been tried. And yet it has not. For many centuries, it has not. The message of this book is that the time is now. The time is now to do something new and yet very old, something different, and yet ever the same, which can be for the good of our time, and for the good of perhaps many generations to come.

www.ingramcontent.com/pod-product-compliance
Lightning Source LLC
Chambersburg PA
CBHW050823160426
43192CB00010B/1879